SEVEN SACRED ATTITUDES®

How to Live in the Richness of the Moment

by

Erica Ross-Krieger

2008
To Ann,
Wishing you a
lifetime of
sacred moments!
All the best,
Erica Ross-Krieger

STILL MOUNTAIN® PRESS

A Still Mountain Press Nonfiction Book

Page design by ImageSupport.com, LLC.
Cover design by Kevin Stock, ImageSupport.com, LLC.

Still Mountain Press, LLC.

Publisher's Cataloging-in-Publication
(Provided by Quality Books, Inc.)

Ross-Krieger, Erica.
Seven sacred attitudes : how to live in the richness of the moment / by Erica Ross-Krieger.
p. cm.
LCCN 2005909660
ISBN 0-9767703-7-7

1. Attitude (Psychology) 2. Self-actualization (Psychology) 3. Conduct of life. I. Title.

BF327.R67 2005 158.1
QBI05-600203

Printed in the United States of America
10 9 8 7 6 5 4 3 2 1

Dedicated with love

to my husband, Steve, who holds open

a space for me in the world.

"This engaging life manual teaches you to rely on Sacred Attitudes to nurture your inner wisdom, cultivate serenity and allow happiness to emerge. Following Erica Ross-Krieger's simple daily process of Stop, Breathe, Notice and Choose will help you focus on the heart-centered present."

ROGER JAHNKE, O.M.D.
Author of *The Healer Within*
and *The Healing Promise of Qi*

"Seven Sacred Attitudes is the road map for those seeking total well-being and balance in their lives, helping them avoid all the modern day pitfalls and learn to be a success in the game of life."

GARY QUINN
Author of *May the Angels Be With You*

"In this personal, heart-full collection of essays, fables, and thought-provoking inquiries, Erica Ross-Krieger invites us to reflect on life's greater purpose and meaning, tap our own intuition and cultivate insights that deepen our understanding of ourselves. Full of practical wisdom that can easily be applied, Seven Sacred Attitudes is a wonderful companion for all spiritual travelers and anyone seeking to enrich the quality of his or her life."

ANN K. LINDSAY
Author, *Watercolor: A New Beginning: A Holistic Approach to Painting*

"I laughed, I cried, I opened my heart, I examined my own attitudes. And in so doing, I moved further along my own path to wholeness. Thank you, Erica Ross-Krieger, for your insights, your humor, and your teachings. This must-read book will light the way for anyone recognizing the need for his or her own 'attitude adjustment' on their sacred path to healing."

PATRICIA J. MEYER, N.D.
Naturopathic Physician
Founder, Namaste Natural Healing Center

"Caution! Reading Erica Ross-Krieger's Seven Sacred Attitudes may change your life. Through a series of entertaining personal essays, each followed by a set of life-expanding questions, she invites us, with gentle yet compelling power, to reflect on the meaning and quality of our daily lives."

A.J. GARROTTO
Author of *Circles of Stone*

"As you savor and contemplate the many delicious gems inside *Seven Sacred Attitudes*, you will find Erica Ross-Krieger has accomplished two marvelous things: first, by sharing her most vulnerable moments, she reveals the Heart of a true Teacher; and second, in entertaining style, she gives us a new model for being with ourselves, coaching others and making our lives full and meaningful. This book is a smorgasbord of delights and a must-read for all those called to awaken their passion."

CRAIG CARR, CPCC, PCC
Founder, Coaching Elements, Inc.
Senior Trainer, Coaches Training Institute

CONTENTS

SEVEN SACRED ATTITUDES

FORWARD

I first met Erica Ross-Krieger when she attended a two-day Taming Your Gremlin® seminar I was conducting in Northern California. I liked Erica immediately and was thrilled when she later applied for the Gremlin Taming™ Institute's Professional Training Program. I'm honored to claim her as a graduate.

Erica's commitment to authenticity is unwavering and she is extremely kind. This is a rare blend and as a result of it there is simple and beautiful elegance to the way Erica relates to people and events. This graceful style is reflected in her work with her clients and seminar participants and, as you will see in *Seven Sacred Attitudes®*, in her writing.

Erica uses entertaining vignettes from her own life to illustrate each of the *Sacred Attitudes*. Because her work is bereft of jargon and stilted concepts, and because she's a wise soul and a damn good writer, you are sure to enjoy this work immensely, to find it useful, and to want to share it with others.

Rick Carson

Author of *Taming Your Gremlin®*

SEVEN SACRED ATTITUDES INTRODUCTION

Some of our attitudes hold us back from being and doing all we are meant to be and do. Some even rob us of the richness of the moment and make our lives more difficult and complicated than necessary.

There are other attitudes that foster meaningful action in our lives, lead to wellbeing, and deepen our learning along the way. I call these attitudes **sacred**.

One definition of the word *sacred* is "worthy of respect." The attitudes that bring us more fully into the world are indeed worthy of our respect.

The small book you hold in your hands is not a book about *positive thinking*. Rather, it's a book about *attitudes*. An attitude is all-encompassing. It includes more than just our way of thinking, it also involves our physical being. Ballet dancers and pilots are very familiar with how comprehensive the word "attitude" is; in their respective fields, "attitude" involves the physical position of the body or an airplane.

To illustrate further, suppose I told you I went to a restaurant last evening where the young waitress had an "attitude." Suppose I also told you that her "attitude" was even more evident when I asked her to bring my salad dressing on the side and my water without ice cubes. Now, if I were to ask you to stand up right now and adopt the actual physical posture of a waitress or waiter with an "attitude," you would know exactly what to do. It would likely involve putting your hand on your hip, rolling your eyes upward, and maybe even clicking your tongue and sighing.

Once we become conscious of our attitudes—how they show up in our thinking and physical being, we become empowered to choose our attitudes.

My first awareness of the full concept of "attitude" came almost 20 years ago when I needed to slow down due to a physical health challenge. As I began to slow down, I noticed that the process involved much more than decreasing motion. Slowing down involved a new way of thinking and a new way of being. In order to slow down in every way, I needed to adopt a new *attitude*.

When I looked up "attitude" in Webster's dictionary, I knew the word was the right one to describe what I was learning—**attitude: a physical posture either conscious or unconscious, (especially) while interacting with others**.

Yes, I thought, *Go Slow* is an "attitude." I *am* different "with others" after adopting the *Go Slow* attitude. I stand at ease, have a different way of thinking, and I behave differently.

I found that I when I was in a *Go Slow* attitude, I saw things I didn't see when I was in a "Go Fast" attitude. I noticed the sweet details of life, like the rhythm of my breath, the way my husband held his pen when he wrote, and how my food tasted.

I learned that it was unrealistic to expect the *Go Slow* attitude to take hold overnight or to set up a permanent camp in my life. Instead, I knew that developing the *Go Slow* attitude meant giving it my conscious attention on a daily basis. I would have to cultivate this attitude, much like a gardener tends crops.

After seeing what a remarkable difference adopting the *Go Slow* Attitude made in my life, I began a conscious journey to discover what other Sacred Attitudes might help me create a more meaningful life.

I began to pay attention to the attitudes I was harboring whenever I felt stuck, and I started to notice the effect different attitudes had on my life. The more aware I was, the more obvious the attitudes became. For example, someone we didn't know well invited my husband and me to a summer barbeque. For weeks before the barbeque, I struggled to remember why we'd said yes. I didn't want to go; I just wanted to stay home and work on an idea I had for this book.

One minute, something deep inside told me to go to the barbeque. A minute later, I found myself thinking the idea was ridiculous and inventing excuses so I wouldn't have to go. The inner battle continued.

And then I stopped. I purposely took a deep breath. I noticed my "attitude"—my physical posture—the way I'd been breathing. I noticed I was scrunching my brow, thinking too much, and holding my breath. I was ignoring the warm and calm feeling inside that was telling me to go to the barbeque.

I purposefully took another deep breath and made a firm choice. I would use my inner wisdom. We would go to the barbeque.

Soon after we arrived, Tom and Julie, a couple we'd known for some time, showed up. We had no idea they'd be there or that they knew the host. Seeing them was a pleasant surprise and reason enough to be glad we came. But there was another surprise.

Later that evening, Tom told us a story about his recent pilot's license exam. The story was about the power of attitudes. (His story is in chapter one.) I was amazed. The story was just what I needed to round out my book idea. I wouldn't have heard it if I'd stayed home.

I realized I had come across another Sacred Attitude: *Use Inner Wisdom*.

There is no mistaking the presence of a Sacred Attitude. Once you allow one to enter into your life, there is more space for your natural self to shine—more room for you to "come to life more fully," as author John G. Sullivan says. I believe there is also more room for *life to come to you more fully*, as it did for me that evening.

During my journey to discover more Sacred Attitudes, I continued my spiritual and psychological studies and expanded them to related fields. I spent time with many great teachers of spirituality, philosophy, somatic emotional psychology, Yoga, nutrition, Tai Chi, and the principles of Chinese Medicine. They have all enriched my life. However, I have found that the greatest lessons of all come from giving daily attention to my attitudes and how they affect my life experience.

Over time, I have found Seven Sacred Attitudes that bring more meaning to my life:

1) Use Inner Wisdom

2) Accept What's So

3) Go Slow

4) Do Less

5) Show Up

6) Trust the Process

7) Be With the Questions

Making these attitudes a regular part of my life has become my top priority. The simple daily process I use for cultivating Sacred Attitudes is:

Stop Breathe Notice Choose

- **Stop** means to do just that.
- **Breathe** means to take a few slow, deep breaths and pay attention to the physical effects.
- **Notice** means to observe the "attitude" I am holding. Am I insisting? Going fast? Fighting for answers? Doubting myself? I notice the physical aspect of my "attitude." Am I wrinkling a brow? Hunching my shoulders? Holding my breath? I notice what is before me. Right here, right now. If it is an emotion, I feel it fully. If it is a burned roast or a frozen computer, I just notice it (after I notice my screaming).

- **Choose** means to take an action that supports one of the Seven Sacred Attitudes I want to cultivate. **Use Inner Wisdom. Accept What's So. Go Slow. Do Less. Show Up. Trust the Process. Be With the Questions**. I might choose to stop rushing, and to *Go Slow*. I might choose to stop insisting, to experiment, and *Accept What's So*.

Stop Breathe Notice Choose

This daily practice is simple to do when all is right with the world. It is not so simple when we're faced with the challenges of our daily life or when in the face of tragedy. But if you've become accustomed to cultivating the Sacred Attitudes in the less challenging moments, it becomes easier to cultivate them in the hardest of circumstances. Cultivating Sacred Attitudes is an ongoing practice. We do the best we can do each moment in our lives.

You'll notice that I use many stories in this book to encourage you to explore and practice the Seven Sacred Attitudes. As Barry Lopez's fable, *Crow and Weasel*, teaches, "*stories are the way we care for one another and they are the bread for our journeys*."

Stories can show us that we have options and that there are places for us to test out new attitudes. New postures. New ways of thinking and being in the world. And this is where the fun starts.

Each of my stories represents one of the Seven Sacred Attitudes in action. The inquiries—powerful questions to ponder—that follow each essay are meant to help you reflect on the message of that story and see how it applies to your own life.

Use the stories and inquiries for inspiration. Use them for introspection. Use them for discussion groups with friends. Use them to help you cultivate the Seven Sacred Attitudes in your life.

Erica Ross-Krieger
Walnut Creek, California
December 2005

SACRED ATTITUDE ONE
USE INNER WISDOM

I have an inner compass.

—Julia Cameron

You cannot listen to the God of your heart,
while you are busy monitoring the god of opinion.

—Dan Millman

Why do you weep? The source is within you...

—Rumi

Every day we are bombarded with images, advertisement slogans and magazine articles telling us how to care for our bodies, minds, careers and pocketbooks. With these daily reminders that something or someone outside of us knows what we need and what is best for us, it's no wonder that many of us are confused—we even wonder what foods to eat and what colors to wear. And to alleviate the confusion, we ask "experts" to guide us.

But sole reliance on what others think is a pricey habit to adopt. Like the sounds of static from a poor cellular phone connection, too many opinions cause us to forget where true wisdom resides—keep us from hearing our own inner wisdom.

We can put aside the crackling and confusing sounds of external opinions and tune in to another channel. All we have to do is stop and take a breath.

It's true.

When we stop and take a breath, we make room for the still, small voice of our inner wisdom. We also make room for hearing what our own bodies tell us. Our own breath, the center of our physical being, the breath of life that connects us to all living things, is part of us all the time. Taking a breath is the first step in tuning in to our inner wisdom.

More than Intuition

The first Sacred Attitude, *Use Inner Wisdom*, reminds us that inner wisdom resides in our hearts and in our bodies, for inner wisdom is more than intuition. It lives in the cells of our bodies. Those cells contain volumes of wisdom—from past physical training we've had, to knowledge of what foods are best for us.

In the health realm, for example, once we have taken a deep breath and tuned in to the channel of our own being—our Inner Wisdom channel—we can put conscious attention to our actions and ask ourselves questions such as "What health routine works for me?" "How does my body feel about Yoga, skiing, or broccoli?" "How does that morning coffee make me feel?" "How does my body *feel* after inhaling a cigarette?" Then we can adopt the

Sacred Attitude, *Use Inner Wisdom*, and listen to what our bodies have to say about our actions.

This Sacred Attitude, *Use Inner Wisdom*, also begs us to listen to our internal wisdom in other realms (financial, career, relationships.) When we do, we may be surprised by what we learn. For example, let's say that you're struggling with a decision about a financial investment. You might **Stop**—go outside, stand and stretch, give yourself a break. Then **Breathe**—take a few deep breaths. Take a minute to **Notice**—check out your "attitude"—and be a fair witness to what you observe. "Hmm, my stomach is in knots, my breathing's been shallow for hours and I have a headache; I have solid, positive information about the XYZ stock—from the advisor *and* from my own research; and at the same time, I have a strong, intuitive sense that this isn't the right stock for me." Finally, you **Choose**—choose to *Use Inner Wisdom* and see what happens. "I think I will *Use Inner Wisdom and trust*—I have to let this stock go."

For some of us, the inner wisdom we seek is revealed to us through bodily sensations. Our guts rumble when we think about changing jobs. For others, inner wisdom is a quiet knowing. No matter what the form is for you, the first step in accessing inner wisdom is to stop and take a deep breath.

Begin Now

Something greater than we are put the gift of inner wisdom inside each of us. Our job is to access that inner wisdom and put the wisdom to use. As a global community, we need each person on the planet to adopt the Sacred Attitude, *Use Inner Wisdom*. And we can begin right now...with the next breath we take.

The essays and inquiries in this section invite you to access your own inner wisdom—to listen to the wisdom of your heart and body.

So, go ahead.

Begin now.

Breathe.

Then, listen.

Your *Inner Wisdom* is waiting to speak.

RECOVERY FROM UNUSUAL ATTITUDES

Some evenings are more memorable than others. There is one I will never forget. It was the 4th of July and my husband and I were attending an evening barbeque at a friend's home in the Berkeley hills. But it wasn't the gourmet food, the sweet evening air, or the brilliant fireworks display that took my breath away. It was the story I heard.

Between bites of potato salad, our friend, Tom, told us about his recent accomplishment. He had just added his instrument rating to his private pilot's license and was still excited about having done so. He told us:

> "The day before my final Instrument Flight Rules check, I went out to the airstrip to get some more practice. I'd hired my instructor to fly with me for a few hours. He was also the FAA examiner who'd be with me for the check the next day, so I knew I'd get some good feedback.
>
> "I climbed into the left seat of the Cessna I'd rented and my instructor, Bill, sat beside me. He told me to take the plane up to five thousand feet, and that he'd instruct me further once we got there.
>
> "When we reached the altitude he'd indicated, Bill's instructions surprised me. 'I'll be taking over the controls here, Tom. I want you to close your eyes.'
>
> "I was scared as hell. But I trusted him, and so I

did as he instructed.

"'Just sit tight, Tom. I'll let you know when I need you to open your eyes and take over again.'

"First, I could feel the plane climbing higher and then level out. I had no idea what Bill was planning.

"The next thing I knew, the motor turned fewer rpm's and the plane slowed down. I heard the familiar 'click, click' as Bill flipped switches and changed settings. But that wasn't all he did.

"There are two sets of rudder pedals in the plane that are connected to each other. Since I could feel the set moving beneath my feet, I knew Bill was also manipulating the rudder.

"I could tell that the plane was turning to the right. I felt the left wing rise. The plane stayed that way just a little too long for my liking. I was dying to open my eyes. My hands began to get sweaty and I felt a bit queasy. The nose was up also and I knew that if Bill didn't make a correction soon, the flight of that airplane could go into distress.

"Then Bill said, 'She's all yours, now, Tom. Get this plane stabilized.'

"I opened my eyes and my panic turned to terror. We were in the midst of a cloud and I didn't know which way was up. I had to rely on the instrument panel. In that instant I realized this was the test.

"My fear didn't leave, but somewhere in the

midst of my panic I found myself flying the plane and just...breathing. With each breath, I found all my flight lessons were there for me. I did what I had to do. Before I knew it, I had stabilized the plane and was flying straight and level.

"Bill smiled. 'Nice work, Tom. Now do a steep 720-degree turn to the left and come out on a heading north. Then do the same thing to the right. After that, descend from this cloud cover.'

"I did the rest of the required maneuvers he'd instructed and brought us down out of the clouds. I could see the airstrip again. I took the Cessna in for a smooth landing and taxied to the tie downs.

"I turned off the engine and looked at Bill. He shook my hand and said, 'Great job up there, Tom. You passed the test.'

"I breathed a sigh of relief. The whole experience was quite incredible."

"Wow!" I said, when Tom finished the story. "Did the instructor create that situation just for you or does he do it for every pilot's instrument flight test?"

"Oh, that's a regular test," Tom said. "It's called Recovery From Unusual Attitudes."

"Attitudes?" I said. "I thought the word was *altitude*?"

"No, *attitude* is a term that means the relative position of the plane to the horizon. When the wings are level and the nose is parallel to the horizon, you're in a stable flying configuration. When you execute a maneuver other than that—make a turn, or lift the nose to go higher—the plane is in what's called an '*unusual attitude*.' If a correction isn't made soon, a hazardous flight condition can occur."

That's when I became speechless. Tom's words struck a deep chord in me—as if a rich, low-pitched gong had gone off inside my head and vibrated through my heart. He didn't know it, but Tom had just given me a gift. In one short story he had summed up my belief in the power of *attitudes*. His words left me in a reflective mood for weeks.

I thought about what it means to have "unusual attitudes" in life and what it takes to recognize them. I realized that we all hold attitudes that cause us distress—ways we make ourselves miserable. How often do we take the time to identify them? I wondered. How often do we make a concerted effort to make "attitude" adjustments and get back to flying straight and level?

Tom's story also caused me to think about the oh-so-familiar attitude of "self-doubt." During his pilot's test, Tom faced that attitude head on. But it was more than his training that helped him move past self-doubt into more important territory. It was his *attitude*—the way he'd he remembered to breathe, focus on the job in front of him, and trust his inner wisdom to access his skills—that helped him bring the plane back to stable flight. His story will always remind me to choose to do the same—to mind my *attitude* and use my inner wisdom.

INQUIRIES:

- **What attitudes keep you flying on course?**
- **Where in your life do you engage the attitude of "self-doubt"?**
- **What support do you need to *Use Inner Wisdom*?**

FIVE DANGEROUS WORDS

One crisp autumn morning, I drove downtown for a breakfast meeting with a client. I hummed along to the oldies music on the radio and found myself smiling.

When I stopped at a red light, I noticed a faint whisper of steam in front of my car. It was rising from the space between my front bumper and the back of the mini-van that stopped in front of me. I figured the source of the steam was the mini-van's warm exhaust meeting with the cold air. So I turned my attention back to the song on the radio.

At the next traffic light, the mini-van scooted through the intersection as the light turned yellow. I caught the red light. As I sat there, I noticed steam-like vapor rising from the hood of my car. But this time there was no mini-van's exhaust pipe in front of me. The cold air against my car's warm engine is causing this vapor, I thought. I glanced at my temperature gauge just in case the engine was more than warm. But the car was fine. The gauge indicated a medium temperature. So on I went.

I found a parking spot, met with my client, and then drove home.

At 6:30 that evening, I got back into my car and headed to my Monday night writing class. At a stop sign along the way, I noticed a faint bit of steam rising from the hood of my car again. I pulled a familiar bit of reasoning from my short-term memory. Okay, it's got to be the cold night air against the car's warm engine that's causing this, I figured. But unconvinced of my logic, I checked the temperature gauge. It said normal. I shrugged, drove on and got to class a few minutes later.

I took my seat and pushed aside any concern about my car's mysterious vapor. I was relieved to focus instead on the writing lesson of the week.

I had an uneventful ride home. When I walked in the door, I mentioned the vapor to Steve. "I'll take a look under the hood for you tomorrow," he said.

A week of tomorrows went by. Neither of us remembered to check under the hood. But I didn't see any vapor that week, either.

So I went on about my business, paying less and less attention to the car's temperature gauge each day. I figured the less I checked the gauge, the less my chances would be of finding anything wrong.

At the end of the week, I drove to my chiropractor's office. I settled into a chair in the waiting room. Not in the mood for thumbing through the old copies of *Reader's Digest* or *People*, I amused myself by looking around the room. I checked the clock on the wall a few times, noticed that the Boston fern was greener than the one I had at home, and stared at the geometric pattern of the blue and white carpet.

Whoops. I turned back to the wall. Something next to the clock had caught my eye. Something I hadn't noticed before—despite the many times I'd been to my chiropractor's office. That *something* was a small, brown, wooden sign:

Five dangerous words:

Maybe it will go away.

The sign was posted to encourage my chiropractor's clients to listen to their bodies and to come in for treatment sooner rather than later. But the sign said much more than that to me that day.

In a flash it told me to attend to that vapor coming out of the hood of my car. And as soon as my appointment was over, I drove straight to the Toyota service department.

I told the attendant on duty about the vapor. One look and she had the mystery solved. "Your radiator is cracked," she told me. "One more mile and it would have overheated. You must know your car pretty well to have come in when you did. It's a good thing you listened to the signs."

She had no idea what *sign* I'd "listened" to.

We each face at least *one* situation in our lives we wish would either go away—disappear with a snap of our fingers and a magic phrase like "presto-change-o"—or be transformed overnight without any intervention on our part. Whether that circumstance is a dissatisfying career, an unrealized dream, a bad marriage, an injustice we don't want to mention, signs of abuse that we'd rather not acknowledge, or a mile high stack of unopened mail—one thing is certain:

Wishing that "maybe it will go away" won't make it so. Only action holds the power of transformation.

INQUIRIES:

- **What are you pretending not to know?**
- **What are you hoping will just go away?**
- **When will you take action?**

BUBBLING SPRING

Hal Bailen, M.D. (1935-1991) was a wise and loving man whose compassion, mastery of acupuncture and gentle kindness brought comfort and healing to many. I was blessed to know him.

Hal began to treat me with acupuncture in 1985, to help me improve my overall health. After three months of treatment, I knew with certainty that Hal's work and wisdom were just what my body and soul needed.

"Hal," I said, at the end of my treatment one spring day, "my physical and emotional stamina has increased since I've been coming to see you."

"Tell me more," Hal said.

I scooted off the treatment table and took a seat on the antique upholstered side chair next to Hal's desk. "Well, as long as I come for treatments each week and keep taking my herbal supplements, I have the energy and strength I need to enjoy a productive day. That wasn't true in January." I bent over to put on my Addidas.

"Hmm. This is not such a good thing," Hal said.

"It's not?"

"Well, it's good that you're stronger," Hal said. "But it's not good that you attribute your increased energy to things outside of you."

I leaned my elbows on Hal's old brown desk. "But aren't the things that are helping me outside of me?"

"Yes and no," Hal said. "Yes, herbs and acupuncture are outside of you but they are not the source of your growing energy and strength."

I squirmed in my seat and wrinkled my brow.

"Let me give you a homework assignment," Hal said, looking at me over the top of his silver bifocals. "Then you tell me what is making you stronger the next time you come."

"Okay." I took a pen and notepaper from my Day Timer.

"There's nothing to write down," Hal said. "Take your right shoe off and lift up your foot."

I untied my laces, took my shoe off again and stuck out my foot.

Hal got down on his knees and held my foot. "Right here, in the middle of the ball of your foot, and toward the center a bit, is the point the Chinese call the Bubbling Spring." Hal pressed his thumb into the spot with a light touch.

"Yup. I feel it all right," I said, smiling through a slight grimace, "but you can stop pressing now."

Hal took his thumb off the spot but continued to hold my foot. "Bubbling Spring is the heart of your sole," he said, as he gave my foot a loving squeeze. "It's located in the same place in your other foot, also."

"Okay. So what's the homework?"

Hal stood up. "Bubbling Spring is a powerful acupuncture point," he said. "But we don't need needles to activate the energy it provides. Each time we step we activate the Bubbling Spring point."

"So I don't need to do anything different? Just walk?"

"Be mindful," Hal said.

"What?"

"This week, be mindful of Bubbling Spring as you walk. Keep

in mind that each time you step you activate a Bubbling Spring of energy that's within you," Hal said. "In other words, you cultivate more of your own Life Energy."

"That's it? That's all I do?"

"That's plenty," Hal said and gave me a hug goodbye.

I walked to my car, paying attention to my steps.

I stayed as mindful as I could of Bubbling Spring that week. Doing so became a challenging game—one that I enjoyed. It also perked me up.

Although I had a few particularly long days that week—in fact, sitting in front of the TV after supper took about all the energy I could muster—I had a new tool. When I sat, I took my shoes off and pressed the Bubbling Spring point. Within short order, a new round of energy kicked in and I was back in action—off to balance the checkbook, clean out a drawer, or start an art project. One night I even organized an entire linen closet. This isn't something I usually have energy to tackle this late at night, I thought, as I moved towels. I knew it wasn't the TV that had perked me up—so I figured I had activated my own energy reserves by massaging the Bubbling Spring point.

Throughout the week, I walked wherever I could. As I did, I imagined that an unlimited supply of energy came bubbling up from my feet. And, somehow, I felt more bounce in my step.

I looked forward to telling Hal what I was noticing—especially about the changes that seemed to be coming as a result of my *attention* on Bubbling Spring as I walked.

Two days before my appointment, Hal's secretary called.

"Erica, Hal has to reschedule your Wednesday session," Susan said. "He can see you next week at the same time, though. Does that work for you?"

"I guess so," I said, checking my calendar. "Hal hasn't rescheduled me the entire three months I've been seeing him," I said. "Does he do that often?"

"To tell you the truth, it's a first since I've worked here," Susan said, "and I've been here a year. It's some personal thing that's come up. But he's seeing clients tomorrow if there's an emergency...is there?"

"No," I said. "I'll be there next week."

I hung up the phone. My neck was knotted with tension. Now what? I really needed those sessions each week to keep me strong and my energy up.

Oops. I stopped.

I took a deep breath.

Then I grabbed a sweatshirt and headed outside for a walk.

As I started down the street, I put my focus on the Bubbling Spring points in my feet.

Within one block, I discovered I could be mindful of my steps and still take in the sweetness of the plum blossoms that decorated the neighborhood trees.

Within two blocks I could sense the powerful energy that seemed to come from the Bubbling Spring of my own steps.

By the time I got home, my shoulders had relaxed and I knew with certainty the source of my healing.

***

The following week, I met with Hal. "Well," he said, "what's the report?"

"That was a great assignment," I said, hopping up onto the treatment table.

"What did you learn?" Hal held my wrist and checked my pulses.

"My own Bubbling Spring showed me that healing energy is right here within me."

Hal smiled.

"I also could feel the earth itself supporting me," I said. "It made me realize I don't have to rely solely on my own willfulness each day—I've got another means of support."

"Sounds like focusing on Bubbling Spring gave you a nice way of connecting to your *soul* through your *sole*," Hal said.

"Sure did. But I *do* have a question, Hal. Did you reschedule my appointment on purpose?"

Hal's eyes twinkled.

INQUIRIES:

- **What will your day be like if you give your attention to your steps?**
- **When you step, what do you notice?**
  - **Are your steps hesitant?**
  - **Are your strides confident?**
  - **Are you pulled up, tight in your chest and unaware of your feet?**
- **What is it to be a Bubbling Spring?**

MAKING LIFE MORE COMFORTABLE

As I sat there, in the stillness of the warm evening sun, sipping cold bottled water and watching the soap splatter my windshield, I smiled to myself. Life had become slower for a moment and much more comfortable.

For years, my Yoga teacher and friend, Ofer, has asked a simple question in Yoga class. Each time we settle into a stretch or pose, he says, "How can you make this more comfortable?" It's an invitation for us to adjust our positions and attain comfort.

A few minutes later Ofer says, "Now, how can you make this same pose even *more* comfortable?" His rich, deep voice and Hebrew accent seem to add to the importance of the question. Once again, we alter our positions—ever so slightly, most of the time—so that our bodies enjoy the postures.

Regardless of what our stretch or posture looks like compared to our Yoga teacher's, we are to find a way to do the postures *our* way—the way that is most comfortable for us that day.

Ofer says the idea behind his question is to get us to see that our bodies respond much more to comfort than to discomfort. He wants us to see that more comfort and more awareness become available to us when we seek more comfort. What a concept.

Here in the Western world, we seem to pride ourselves on making things harder and more difficult, rather than more comfortable. This tendency is apparent *everywhere* we look—not just in gyms and fitness classes. Even as I write this essay I wonder why I am hunched over the keyboard, shoulders tensed, holding my breath.

Some time ago, I thought it would be a good idea to apply Ofer's question to the areas of my life outside of Yoga class—to make a practice of living with his question, "How can I make this more comfortable?"

I did fine for a while. I'd notice I was doing something with some discomfort, make adjustments and then do the same thing with more ease. From adjusting the way I bent to tie a shoe, to disorganizing my wrinkled brow as I talked on the phone with a client, I found lots of ways to make things more comfortable.

I also noticed that by making things more comfortable each day, I had more access to my inner wisdom. For instance, I knew what words to use on a once-troubling writing piece when I sat in a more comfortable position at my desk. When I adjusted my posture at the dinner table, I enjoyed my food more and found that my body just naturally stopped eating when I was full. I guess that my intuition was freed up when my unconscious attention wasn't focused on discomfort and pain.

Then somewhere along the line, my daily practice of making things more comfortable slipped. We bought a new house, moved, and I got caught up in the busy-ness of life. I once again became familiar with the discomfort of stress.

Last summer, my "making it more comfortable" practice clicked in again. It was a warm 97-degree day. Everything I did drained my energy. And I had lots to do that day. In the back of my mind, I knew I had to have enough energy left to get to a not-so-engaging watercolor class at 7:00 that evening.

As 5:30 approached, and my To Do list was still long enough for any two people, I stopped. I slowed down. I took a breath. I waited.

Out of the blue, I remembered to apply Ofer's question to my circumstances. "How can I make my life more comfortable this evening?"

My answer appeared. I found myself saying aloud, "Erica, scratch the watercolor class that you don't enjoy. Your car needs gas and it's filthy, too. Go to the gas station. Then take the car to your favorite car wash place before it closes." I heeded my own words.

When I got to the car wash, I handed the guy my keys. I found a seat outside and sat down. I took a deep breath. I knew right then that hurrying to get dinner together, eating fast, and rushing off to a class that I didn't love was nowhere near comfort.

I realized then, that as often as I could remember I'd ask myself Ofer's question, "How can I make myself more comfortable?"

So, please excuse me while I stop to answer Ofer's question right this minute—I think it's time I un-fold my scrunched-up posture and find a more comfortable way to write the inquiries for this essay—

INQUIRIES:

- **What is difficult about making things easier?**
- **Where does your life want to flow right now?**
- **What beliefs would you have to relinquish to be able to "make life more comfortable" each day?**

SACRED ATTITUDE TWO

ACCEPT WHAT'S SO

One of the first things to do is learn to accept, and to expect this Power to flow through everything we do.

—Ernest Holmes

The real voyage of discovery consists not in seeking new landscapes, but in having new eyes.

—Marcel Proust

Acceptance does not mean fatalism... Those who follow Tao do not believe in being helpless. They believe in acting within the framework of circumstance. For example, in a drought, they will prepare by storing what water is available. That is sensible action. They will not plant a garden of flowers that requires a great deal of water.

—Den Ming-Dao

The mission of the Human Potential movement of the '70s was to wake us up and get us to realize we were responsible for our own lives. Proponents of the philosophy wanted us to understand that we have the greatest power on earth available to us—the power to shift our attitudes. In Human Potential workshops across the nation, we learned that we could use our attitudes to shape our lives. The Human Potential movement was a noble cause.

Insistence vs. Acceptance

But some of us took the notion too far. We mistook the original idea and created an attitude of insistence. "I can do anything and I create everything," we said.

We began believing that with enough insistence we could move actual mountains. But in the midst of this attitude, we forgot to admit that some circumstances are unalterable.

Like the situation our friends, the Bakers, faced when their child came into the world with Down's Syndrome. Insistence did nothing to change the reality of their world.

Something *can* happen with too much insistence, though—several things, in fact—we can create ulcers, heartache, and depression when we insist that the unalterable conditions we face become different from how they are.

The Baker's challenge, my client Doug's recent job loss, and my own health challenge—these circumstances beg for acceptance.

The second Sacred Attitude, *Accept What's So*, reminds us that the energy we expend *insisting*—almost demanding that something were other than it is—can be better spent *accepting*—

dealing with—what is so.

There was a time when we were better at acceptance—a time when we didn't push so hard against the facts. The horse was old and tired, so we put him out to pasture to graze—when we did, the horse helped keep the grass-growth in check. We saw that the milk in the pail had curdled, so we made yogurt and cheese—when we did, we had additional food.

These were times when we didn't *insist*. Instead, we harnessed our energy to *accept* the gifts that unalterable situations held for us.

Webster does a good job describing the difference:

Insist: be firmly demanding

Accept: receive willingly

What is Possible?

The Sacred Attitude, *Accept What's So*, is not an attitude of complacency—it isn't the attitude of a wet doormat. Instead, this Sacred Attitude offers the possibility of transformation.

The first thing the *Accept What's So* attitude asks us to do is step back and look at what is before us.

We aren't required to like what we see nor are we asked to stop pretending a tough situation isn't so tough.

The *Accept What's So* attitude hosts a much bigger conversation than that. This Sacred Attitude has us ask, "What is possible here?"

The essays in this section are snapshots of trying times and situations where acceptance replaces insistence—opening up worlds of possibility.

So take each essay and pretend it is your own story. Pretend it's you in the traffic jam, or you having to cut back on your swimming. Then, consider the inquiries that follow each story. See where the stories and inquiries take you.

Enjoy the journey.

DON'T BE A HERO

One spring, not long ago, the physical symptoms I experience became more challenging. The tingling sensation in my hands and feet was more pronounced, my gait was off and I was walking with a limp. The limping took its toll on me, and caused me to work hard just to walk short distances. Friends, as well as health practitioners, urged me to consider using a cane. But I wouldn't hear of it.

I insisted that true healing meant I would regain leg strength. I was determined to push ahead with my own approach to healing—which didn't include using a cane. I also believed that I was a better wellness coach because I relied on my own strength and pursued my own wellness.

In the summer of the same year, I went to the pool to swim my usual laps. I arrived during off-hours and had a lane all to myself. Soon, I was lost in the rhythm of the swim while my mind wandered back to our spring vacation in Hawaii.

After a while, I looked to my side and saw a silver-haired gentleman getting into the water in my lane—even though there were five free lanes. Well, I guess I'm going to be sharing, I thought, and continued my laps.

As I swam, I noticed the man was *walking* on his side of the pool lane. He seemed to be exercising his legs. I'd seen others do the same so I made sure I left him ample room whenever I swam past him.

When I finished my laps, I stayed in the water and stood at the end of the lane to rest. As I leaned against the pool wall, the man walked over to me.

"Hi," he said, "my name is Ed. I'm here to strengthen my hip before surgery."

I introduced myself and told Ed I thought he was smart to keep exercising his hip.

He said, "I'm eighty. All I want is to live at least five more years and be able to go for morning walks with my lovely wife of sixty years. I'll do whatever I have to in order to make that happen."

Ed was new to the pool and must have thought most people used it for rehab, because he then asked me, "What reason brings *you* here?"

I thought about saying I was just there to swim, but for some reason I felt like answering him in a way that wasn't, and still isn't, typical for me.

Surprised at myself, I said, "Well, Ed, I have MS symptoms and I'm here for exercise."

For the most part, I don't use the MS label. Too many people assume they know the prognosis. They make assumptions and wind up adding to my own anxiety. So, I don't bother with it. Plus, I think of myself as healthy and like to affirm that. This time, however, I felt like it didn't matter what anyone else thought. I could also tell Ed was someone with an understanding heart.

"Oh, you must know Tim," Ed responded, "Tim has MS."

Ahh, I thought, another reason not to use this label. People must think there's a club and all the people who have had an MS diagnosis know each other.

After a brief moment of sarcastic thoughts, I put my attention back on Ed's heart and intention. I said, "No, Ed, I don't know Tim."

"Tim walks with a cane," he said. "Do you?"

"No, I don't," I said. Then I surprised myself again by adding, "I've thought about it though."

To this day, I have no clue why I said that—I hadn't been thinking any such thing. In fact, quite the opposite was true—I was determined to keep walking under my own steam, no matter how tough it was to do so.

Ed got quiet for a minute. Then he turned to look at me with eighty years of wisdom shining through his blue eyes. As if reading my mind, he said, "Life is too short. Don't be a hero." He turned and continued walking his laps.

Many say that whatever we need to hear, or learn, will come to us no matter what—that if we are ready and receptive, the lesson just shows up. "Don't be a hero," was all Ed had to say to me that day, but his words, and the moment, were magic. I began to think about the notion of being a hero, and my insistence that I couldn't coach other people about wellness if I used a cane.

I also began to consider that, to me, being a hero really meant having the courage to accept how things were, even when they were different from how I wanted them to be.

A few weeks after meeting Ed at the pool, I decided to get a cane. Ed's words and my own attitude-shift helped me realize that a cane was simply a tool—a tool I needed to help me live a more joyful and full life. I figured, Hell, if I cut my finger, I'd go get a Band-Aid—this is no different—a Band-Aid's a tool—so is a cane.

Off I went to the pharmacy. I tried out a few canes in the store, found one that met my need, bought it and left.

I practiced with the cane on the way to the car and was quick to learn how to use it. I didn't need to lean on it much. I only needed to touch the cane lightly to the ground, as a means of getting feedback from the earth back to me. The light touch of the cane to the ground helped reassure me—important because I sometimes can't feel much through the numbness and tingling in my feet.

The moment I used the cane in this way, I experienced a sense of ease and freedom. Oh, I thought, now I can look around at the trees and take my eyes off the ground.

I didn't realize how much I missed the trees.

***

Over time, I have come to an inner-directed definition of wellness—one that does not include trying to "tough it out" to be a hero—one that does include accepting what is so.

Thanks, Ed.

INQUIRIES:

- **Where in your life are you insisting that things should be or look a certain way?**
- **What situation in your life needs your acceptance?**
- **What does it mean to you to be courageous?**
- **Where in your life would it be helpful to take in the words of others?**
- **What gifts are present in your life that you haven't made time to appreciate?**

THE PERSPECTIVE SONG

One day, not long ago, I decided to re-read the attitude-changing philosophy in *A Course in Miracles*. Three years before, in its simple to follow lesson-a-day, the Course had helped me cultivate new levels of inner peace. I figured I could use more of the same. Within the first few weeks, I came upon a lesson that showed me I'd figured well.

The lesson was: "There is another way of looking at this."

I reminded myself of the Course's suggested approach for learning—apply each lesson as often as possible throughout the day, to whatever situation is before you. Okay, I thought. Simple enough. I'll go apply "There is another way of looking at this," throughout my day. No problem.

The trouble was that every situation I faced that day was challenging. And there was not another damn way to look at things, thank you very much.

From a crashed computer to people not being available on the phone, to running out of shampoo in the middle of a late-in-the-day shower, my day was filled with frustrating circumstances. The day held little, if any, opportunity for me to look at things anew. And no New Age self-help affirmation was going to convince me otherwise!

So I pulled on my panty hose, zipped up my skirt, dried my un-shampooed wet hair, and left for an appointment that was only twenty minutes away. Or so I thought.

Okay, the traffic is always hellish at the *end* of a workday—but I did *not* expect a bumper-to-bumper gridlock in the middle of the afternoon. Sitting there in my car, I did my best to repeat the day's lesson to myself, hoping that I could find "another way of looking at this" freeway parking lot.

After an eternity, I decided there was no way out and that I'd be better off letting go of my plans and forgetting about making the appointment on time. One cell-phone call later, assuring my colleague that I'd meet her the following day instead, I sat back in the car to wait things out.

As I did, something caught my attention at the side of the road. Pulled over onto the shoulder of the highway was an old, yellow, Ford pickup truck. It was lopsided. When I looked closer, I could see that the front tire was as flat as the terrain in Texas. Since I wasn't moving anywhere, I had plenty of time to stare.

The driver of the truck was sitting on the rusted and beat-up tailgate. He was a young man with a ponytail, wearing well-splattered painter's pants and a matching, torn t-shirt. While waiting for a tow truck, I supposed, or perhaps some divine intervention, he had pulled out his guitar and was moving his mouth as if in song.

I rolled down my window. He was singing at the top of his lungs. My mouth hung open as I looked closer and saw the peace on his face.

He'd found "another way of looking at this." His music made me smile. His attitude cleared the traffic jam in my head.

I think he understood the lesson for the day.

At last, I did too.

INQUIRIES:

- **What is frustrating you right now?**
- **What are some other possible perspectives on this situation? (How would a child see it? How would it be written in a novel?)**
- **What gifts does the situation hold for you?**

AS I AM

I woke up with a smile on my face. I knew I had a light schedule ahead of me that day, and not a care in the world. I padded off to the bathroom, focused on the joy of a morning shower.

I turned the shower on and stepped into the hot, steamy oasis. The strong spray of water felt delicious on my skin. I stood still for several minutes, enjoying the sensation. Then I reached for the liquid shower-gel and a scrubbie sponge, and bent over to lather my right leg.

I started from my foot and worked my way up over my calf and thigh muscles. Boy, this leg feels so strong, I thought, enjoying the feeling of my muscles against the sponge. I love the way the lather hugs the taught, healthy skin of this leg. I straightened my leg, then bent it again, and smiled as I noticed the muscle definition. Consistent swimming was paying off.

I began to use the scrubbie on my left leg. I started at my foot, moved to my calf and landed on some thoughts that were mixed in with the lather. Oh, this leg isn't very strong. The muscles are weaker. This leg doesn't hold as much of my weight as it should. Poor leg.

All of a sudden, I stopped lathering and came to a complete halt—not moving, bent over my left leg, the spray of the shower on my back—aghast and amazed.

Somewhere along the way, I'd stopped enjoying the experience of lathering. Somewhere along the way I'd stopped enjoying the experience of the shower. Somewhere along the way

I'd been judging my legs. And I'd been judging my left leg as if it wasn't as good as my right.

I stood up. Then, aloud, I said, "My God, what would happen if I loved this leg just as it is? What if I honor its weakness? In fact, what if I don't label it as being weak? What if I love the muscles in *this* leg and don't compare it to my right leg? What if I love the sensation of scrubbing *this* leg? What if I stop waiting until it gets *stronger*, gets *better* or becomes *different* from how it is now?"

I put down the scrubbie, rinsed off the remaining lather and continued to imagine. What if I live my life like this? What if I love myself just like *I am*? What would my life be like? What if my appreciation for myself, as *I am*, becomes a celebration NOW rather than *someday*? My God, my entire life would change!

Just as I had this epiphany, I found myself standing in the shower more balanced on BOTH of my legs than I had been for a long time.

For years I'd defined health as a feeling of wholeness, not the absence of disease. But I *experienced* my definition of health that morning in the shower in a way that forever changed my life. And I know that lessons like this make my life's journey rich and meaningful.

INQUIRIES:

- **What needs your honoring right now?**
- **What needs to be *included* in the tapestry of your life, rather than dismissed?**
- **In what way would choosing this perspective change things?**

YOU ARE NOT ON THE ROAD TO...

I'd attended a day-long meeting in San Francisco and was anxious to get out of the city before the rush hour—I looked forward to getting home, grabbing my gym bag and going for a swim—so I jumped in my car and all but peeled out of the parking garage.

I headed for the entrance ramp to the Bay Bridge—the one that I thought was right down the block from me. An entrance was there all right, but not the one I wanted. Before I could correct my mistake, I found myself driving up the carpool-only lane toward the bridge.

It wasn't my lucky day. No sooner did I figure out that I was in the wrong place, than a hungry-looking California Highway Patrolman pulled me over. My explanation meant nothing. My tears meant less. The officer didn't care that I'd made an unintentional turn onto the carpool ramp. Satisfying his violation quota, he gave me a two-hundred-dollar ticket.

When I got home and looked at the ticket's fine print, I saw that good fortune was mine after all. I could avoid the fine and clear the error from my driving record. The price? Two days at traffic school.

By computer, I discovered a traffic-school class that met at a nearby hotel. The website said the class was run by a group of comedians and improvisational actors. I hoped their comedic material was good and, since it was sanctioned by the DMV, I signed up.

Day number one of the program seemed to last for weeks. The

jokes were dry and the room was packed and stuffy.

The majority of my classmates were adolescents with chips on their shoulders. While most of them had been caught speeding, their indifference and whining let the instructor know they didn't think they deserved to be there. I had a major headache that night.

It took all my reserve to leave for class the next day, but the certificate of completion was a huge motivator, so off I went. Turns out, I'm glad I did.

The morning lecture was about the dangers of road rage. Some charming kid in baggy pants and heavy ear metal said, "But if some guy, like, cuts me off on the freeway, doesn't use his signal, and then tailgates the guy in front of him, shouldn't I, like, do my part and honk at him, or flash my lights, or try to cut him off to show him how stupid he was?" A number of his peers shook their pierced heads in agreement and looked to see what the instructor would say to that brilliant question.

No response. The room got quiet. And then there it was—the lesson I'd come to hear. The instructor bellowed, **"YOU ARE NOT ON THE ROAD TO TEACH OTHER PEOPLE LESSONS."**

I think the kid got it. At least he heard it.

No one said a word.

The instructor sent us all on a long lunch break.

I sat with his little inspirational message for the rest of the day. In the moments between the parking quiz and the Driver's Bingo game, I continued to ponder the morning's lesson. I thought of the many teachers and books I'd read that say we are all teachers and students of one another. I thought about how those same teachers and books say that just by showing up we often serve as providers of lessons. But teaching lessons we think others *need* to learn is another story, I thought.

I went home in a contemplative mood.

When I walked in the door, my husband was watching a football game. My contemplative mood shifted in a flash. "Damn it, Steve. You should be outside. It's a beautiful day. There are a million things that need attention around here—the yard's a mess, the garage door squeaks—why aren't you—"

In the midst of my screaming, I stopped. I took a deep breath. I noticed I'd gone on automatic. I was acting like the world police, proclaiming the "shoulds" for the day. There I was on the road of life, insisting on teaching someone else a lesson. But my job was to mind my own affairs. Hadn't I just heard that?

Steve stared at me as I stopped in mid-tirade. "Aren't you going to finish the speech?" he said.

"No, I just got back from traffic school and learned a few things." I sighed, shrugged and left the room.

I realized I could save a hell of a lot of energy in my life if I put away my imaginary siren and flashing lights, and remembered that I'm not on the road to teach other people lessons. I'd be better off accepting people as they are and minding my own business—the business of applying life's lessons to myself. Even those from traffic school.

INQUIRIES:

- **Where do you waste precious energy and insist that others do things your way?**
- **What is it to be gentle with yourself? With others?**
- **Who in your life needs you to cut them some slack?**

WHAT'S SO...

"Sue," I said to my editor, "I read a great magazine article—a fable, actually—that I just love. It's a perfect illustration of one of the Sacred Attitudes. I want to include it in my book, but there's a problem."

"What's that?" Sue said.

"Well, I have permission to use the fable," I said, "but it wasn't written exactly the way I would write it."

"Oh?"

"No. I'd break it into more paragraphs. Give the whole thing more space. Can I rewrite it the way I want and credit the magazine anyway?"

"Sorry, Erica," Sue said. "The story was written the way it was written—that's what's so. Either use it or don't. But no changes allowed."

"Oh. I see."

I hung up the phone and typed the story exactly as it appeared in the magazine:

The Crowded Alley

There was once an exceedingly bad-tempered horse tied up by its owner in a narrow alley, blocking passage. The first villager encountering this impasse tried to push past the horse's massive haunches and found himself crushed against the wall. A second tried to jump over the horse's bucking hooves, only to be sent sailing. Another tried to crawl under the horse's belly and was promptly kicked into the dirt. The crowd of villagers grew and tempers flared as one by one they tried to force their way through, only to be thwarted by the increasingly agitated horse.

Suddenly a young child came running excitedly down the alley. Master Keng was approaching from the main road. Surely he would know how to deal with the situation! As Master Keng rounded the corner, he peered down the alley, assessed the situation and smiled as he quietly turned and proceeded to the next alley, continuing calmly on his way.

—*Traditional Chinese Medicine World*

I finished typing, shrugged my shoulders and grinned in surrender—learning to *Accept What's So* was going to be a life-long process.

INQUIRIES:

- **Which "agitated horses" are you attempting to change?**
- **If you were the "Master Keng" in your own life, which alleys would you leave behind?**
- **What is it to "continue calmly on your way"?**

WHAT'S RIGHT WITH ME?

Last year, our friends, Sherry and Don, hosted a special evening-event at the independent bookstore they own. The purpose of the hour-and-a-half gathering was to listen to their friend, Matthew, a gifted intuitive, give readings for those in attendance. The fee was minimal and we'd heard Matthew was quite talented, so we went.

When we arrived, we picked up our nametags at the front desk, helped ourselves to tea and milled around to meet the other people who'd come that evening.

As we schmoozed, we learned that the twenty-or-so people assembled at the bookstore had very diverse backgrounds—Mai Lin, the elder in the crowd, was a great-grandmother and a retired nurse from China; Peter, in his mid-30's, was an electrical repairman for a local public utility company; and Joseph, silver-haired, ebony-skinned and age hard-to-guess, was a minister, visiting from South Africa.

The common thread among us was that we'd each come with important life questions we wanted Matthew to address. We'd brought them in notebooks, in our hearts and on our minds.

At 7:30, Sherry and Don called us all to our seats and welcomed us to the event. Then, after a brief overview of his experience as an intuitive, Matthew began to take questions from the group.

Joseph, the minister, raised his hand and stood as he asked the first question of the evening. "Yes, please," he said, in a gentle South African accent, "what is the best thing I can do for the people of my ministry at this time?"

Matthew was silent for a moment. Then he smiled and said, "Loving them is all that is required of you, Joseph."

Joseph's coffee-colored eyes filled with tears. "I understand," he said, beginning to sit back down.

Matthew coughed and motioned to Joseph to stay standing. "But Joseph," Matthew said, "the greater question is this: How will you love yourself this year? Please think on this question."

Joseph smiled through his tears and sat down with a satisfied sigh.

Wow, I thought. *How will I love myself this year?* What a great question to savor. I tucked it away in my heart and also jotted it down in my notebook.

As the evening unfolded, and Matthew interacted with additional members of the group, I added more notes to my collection—mental as well as written—they were grist for the mill when I returned home and could process things. By 8:30, I found my heart was quite full and my hand was tired from writing. So I closed my notebook, leaned over and whispered to Steve, "I'm not going to bother asking Matthew a question tonight—I just don't think I can take in any more information."

Steve shrugged. "Me, neither," he said, "I've gotten more than enough."

No sooner did I think I was through absorbing lessons, when Stacy, a wholesome-looking teenaged girl with waist-length red hair, vibrant beauty, and wearing a gold USC Athletic Department t-shirt, raised her hand.

Matthew nodded to her.

Stacy unfolded her tall, willowy frame and stood. She wrinkled her freckled brow and said, "Matthew, all my life I've had health challenges."

"Yes, dear," Matthew said, "and, what is your question?"

Stacy narrowed her blue eyes. "I've been to experts from one end of the state to the other," she said, "and no one can figure out what is wrong with me. I just—" She started to cry.

I leaned forward in my seat. My own health had been on my mind and I was curious to see where this was going.

"Take your time," Matthew said, passing a box of tissues down the aisle to Stacy. "Whenever you are ready, continue."

Stacy took a tissue, dabbed her eyes and pushed back her long hair. Then she took a deep breath.

So did the rest of us.

"I just know with my whole heart that if I could just figure out what is *wrong* with me, I could also figure out how to solve my health problems...and then I could get on with my life. What do you think?"

Matthew might have answered, but I didn't hear him. Instead, the echo of Stacy's words, "...figure out what is *wrong* with me...*then* I could get on with my life," filled my head.

I sat back in my seat and rubbed my temples.

A voice from somewhere in my heart wanted to scream out, "Stacy, how would it be if you focused on what is *right* with you—*already* right with you—and started doing so right *now* rather than *someday*?" But I held myself back.

Instead, I took a deep breath. I opened my notebook again and wrote myself a note:

Focus on what is right with me.

I recall very little about the rest of the evening event. But I had plenty to talk about on the way home.

"What did you learn for yourself tonight?" Steve said, backing the car out of the parking lot.

"Stacy taught me so much."

"Like what?"

"Remember when she said she had to figure out what was *wrong* with her?"

Steve stopped at a red light and looked at me. "Yeah. And that taught you what, exactly?"

"Well. Dozens of health practitioners through the years have asked me to keep journals of my physical symptoms—of what's *wrong* with me" I said.

"Yes. But hasn't that been useful?"

"Uh-huh. It's been good to note what is so. But Steve, I've had enough practice focusing on what's *wrong* with me. There's more to acknowledge than that."

"Oh?" Steve smiled.

"Yeah. I'm out of practice focusing on what is *right* with me—physical things and otherwise."

"Hmm," Steve said, as the light turned green. "That's food for thought for all of us."

We drove the rest of the way home in silence.

After I kicked off my shoes, brushed my teeth and donned my favorite old flannel nightgown, I sat in bed and opened my journal. I wanted to begin making a list of all that was right with my body and my entire being.

I titled my list, *What's Right With Me?*

Then I sat there, pen in mid-air, and couldn't think of a single thing to put on the list. This was going to be like exercising forgotten muscles. I guess I'll have to think of tonight's list as a warm-up period and take it easy, I told myself.

And so, one awkward word at a time, I began.

- *My hair is healthy*
- *My nails are strong*
- *I love deeply*
- *I am quite creative*

I read the list. Hmm, this was going to take practice. It was also taking time—Steve had climbed into bed beside me and was already asleep.

With pen back to paper, I considered the question again. *What's right with me*?

I added ten more items in rapid succession. Huh. This is getting easier, I thought. I'll bet tomorrow's list will be even easier.

Happy with my efforts, I read over my first *What's Right With Me* list with a full heart—then I closed my journal for the night.

As I stayed focused on what was *right* with me, I shut the light, slid down in the warm covers and turned to kiss my sleeping husband's cheek. Many things were *right* in my world.

***

So, Stacy, if you're reading this, I wish you all the best in getting on with your life—but please...don't wait. Turn your attention to all that is good and true and whole in you right now. Be well.

INQUIRIES:

- **What is good and true and whole about you right now?**
- **What would it be like to view physical symptoms as your body's best effort at correction and therefore a statement that things are *right* with it?**
- **In his version of the ancient book, *The I Ching*, Brian Browne Walker writes, "*To resolve a difficult situation, start with what is good in yourself.*" What changes for you when you apply this wisdom to a difficult situation?**

SACRED ATTITUDE THREE

GO SLOW

You must learn to be still in the midst of activity and to be vibrantly alive in repose.

—Indira Gandhi

The religious writer and poet Thomas Merton (1915-1968) wrote that when we succumb to busyness and overwork, we actually give birth to a subtle form of violence that destroys our own inner capacity for peace and the fruitfulness of our own work, because it kills the root of inner wisdom that makes work fruitful. But when we slow down, even the most mundane task can become an enjoyable meditation.

—Ann K. Lindsay, *Watercolor: A New Beginning*

We spend most of our time and energy in a kind of horizontal thinking. We move along the surface of things...[but] there are times when we stop. We sit still. We lose ourselves in a pile of leaves or its memory. We listen and breezes from a whole other world begin to whisper.

—James Carroll

Everywhere we turn we are encouraged to adopt the "Go Fast" attitude. Trouble is, while we are crossing more things off of our To Do lists, we are often missing the beauty of the moment.

The third Sacred Attitude, *Go Slow*, invites us to take back those moments. The *Go Slow* attitude acknowledges that we are human beings and not computers—that we don't have high-speed processors inside—that we will never be that fast.

Thank God.

We practice the *Go Slow* attitude each time we say "no" to multi-tasking and "yes" to the one thing that is before us. Even for one minute in the day.

The *Go Slow* attitude is also about learning to stay slow on the inside while we tackle external tasks that require speed. For example, the Go Slow attitude invites us to pay attention to our breath while we are rushing to meet business deadlines—or to stop and smell the fruits and vegetables while we are racing down the aisle with our grocery carts.

Nature's Invitation

We have a lot to learn from nature about the *Go Slow* attitude. Nature invites us to *Go Slow* and pay attention to the moment before us. Trees don't change color in one day. They take a full season. Animals don't keep busy 24/7—they rest—they stop action for a while and replenish.

Both nature and the *Go Slow* attitude invite us to bring all of ourselves to the table of life—all of our attention, all of our senses, and all the intelligence of our bodies, minds and spirits. Have you ever seen a dog dig for a bone? All of him, including his attention, is digging for the bone. He is not worrying about his To Do list at the same time. Digging is a full, joyous event for the dog.

Can you imagine what your life would be like if you were to *Go Slow* and bring your full attention to each moment?

When I *Go Slow* I am always amazed to find there is much more to the moment than I suspected—gifts I wasn't anticipating—like the surprise fragrance of the lavender blooming outside my front door that I can smell when I stop long enough on my way out. I've learned that if I *Go Slow* and give myself to the moment before me, there is room for many hidden blessings to show up.

<u>Fast Pace</u>

It takes courage to *Go Slow*—to go against the addictive fast pace of the world—for us to take a moment for ourselves. It also takes courage to *Go Slow* and face the moments that are downright painful—the moments that take us to the bottom of the ocean floor of our souls.

But how often do we let ourselves go there?

How often, instead, do we find ourselves whitewater rafting on the fast-paced currents of life, trying to stay afloat?

How often do we numb ourselves with the drug of hurry-up-and-get-it-done intensity rather than choosing to *Go Slow* and experience the joy or the sorrow of the moment or day?

I think we are better off embracing the *Go Slow* attitude. We are better off going to the ocean floor of our souls and crying a bit if that's what is ours to do at the time. We are better off staying with the simple pleasure of watching our children learn to skate instead of rushing to check-off as yet another item on our To Do lists. We are better off when we *Go Slow* and fully enter the moment—because the moment changes us.

The essays in this section invite you to *Go Slow* and savor the full, rich experience of each moment—to *Go Slow* and let more of each moment touch you—to *Go Slow* and discover the gift that each moment holds for you. As you receive these essays, enjoy the process of reading them and be open to the gifts they just might have for you.

Go ahead. *Go Slow.*

MARGE'S REQUEST

I met Marge for tea last Friday. We hadn't seen each other for a year. We talked of old times, our families, new projects, and our relationships with our peri-menopausal bodies. We only had an hour together, but between sips of Ginger Peach tea and laughter we somehow managed to do a year's worth of catching up.

Afterwards, we walked toward our cars together. We neared my car first. Unlike my last get-together with Marge, this time I was leaning on a cane as I walked. And I felt rather awkward as I did.

I was noticing my awkwardness when Marge said, "Erica, I'd really like to go for a walk with you some day. Your walking pace is so nice, and slow, and graceful—it's a pace I'd like to walk."

The moment she said this, I could feel my cheeks get warm from my sudden panic. I thought, God, walking outdoors alone is tough enough some days, let alone walking while I try to have a meaningful conversation. When I'm outside, I watch for uneven surfaces as I walk. Unless I'm with Steve, or someone else who understands my need to concentrate on my steps, going for a walk—and talking at the same time—takes so many brain cells the walk becomes stressful.

I opened my car door. I didn't offer any dates I'd be available for a walk. Instead I just said, "Call me. Let's meet for tea again the next time we're both in Berkeley." Then we hugged goodbye and I got in my car. I drove away, alone with my thoughts and Marge's request sitting on the seat beside me.

If Marge and I went for a walk together, I imagined, I'd have to speed up to keep up with her. My cheeks got hot again. "Forget it," I said to the not-so-empty passenger's seat. "I'd rather go slow and walk alone."

A few days later, after some tears, reflection, and a few deep breaths, I uncovered a new thought: Marge didn't ask me if I wanted to go for a brisk walk with her. She asked me if she could go for a slow walk with me. At *my* pace. I stretched my thinking. Would I be giving the world a gift if I invited others to slow down and be quiet with me?

Until the afternoon I met with Marge, I thought I had to speed up to fit into the world around me. It never dawned on me that I *could* invite the world to slow down with me—and that people would want to do so.

Yes, Marge, come and walk with me.

INQUIRIES:

- **When you slow down, what shows up?**
- **If you stopped trying to fit into the world, and let the world fit in with you, what gift might the world come to know?**

AUTUMN LEAVES

Early each evening, at sunset, my husband and our late Golden Retriever, Socrates, went for walks together. Steve didn't take Socrates out for a walk—they took each other. They were a pack. Year in and year out, for nine years, they took part in a ritual.

For Socrates, evening walks were a chance to romp and play. For Steve, evening walks were a time for slowing down.

During the fall, while Socrates romped through piles of dried leaves, Steve often searched for one special leaf to take home to me. He'd always look for a fallen leaf that was bright and varied in color—a leaf that still held the green of summer along with the crisp red and golden yellow of its new fall wardrobe. Those leaves were splendid.

Even though I didn't go along for those sunset walks—evenings found me doing artwork, writing, or resting—each fall I had an active role in the after-walk ritual. My part was to receive the leaves Steve brought home...and to get a lick from Socrates.

Choosing a leaf for me was Steve's way of slowing down enough to see the important things. Receiving the leaves—and my dog's sweet kiss on my cheek—helped me see the important things, too.

Socrates gave me his final lick in the spring before we moved into our new house. During our first fall without our four-legged friend, Steve continued his evening ritual anyway—at sunset, he'd go for a walk and bring home a beautiful leaf for me.

As the years have gone by, and our routines have changed, Steve's evening walks have slowly faded into the background. But he still manages to head out for few of them each fall.

So, even though it is summer now, and the leaves on the neighborhood trees are bright green, I know that some of them will find their way to me when they are brilliant hues of red and gold. Steve will take the time to slow down and go for an evening walk...and I will take the time to slow down and receive the gift of the leaves.

INQUIRIES:

- **What rituals help you slow down?**
- **What is coming to an end for you?**
- **What lingers?**
- **This week, don't look for more things to *do* in order to slow down. Look at what you already do. Perhaps you make your kids hot cocoa on fall evenings. Maybe you make a cup for yourself. Maybe at the end of your day, you put on your favorite sweats...or take a hot bath. A small shift in perspective might help you see that this is your ritual for slowing down. This week, will you honor what you already do?**

BUTTERSCOTCH CANDY

My new Toyota Corolla was parked in the garage and my old car was parked in front of our house with a For Sale sign taped to the back window. I, however, wasn't parked anywhere at the moment. I was driving down the freeway of my life at top speed.

I finished writing for the day and glanced at my watch. Uh-oh, I thought, no time to spare. It was four-thirty and my writing group would be coming to my house in less than three hours. I still had a list of calls to make, a half-hour phone session with a coaching client, dinner to prepare, and a mountain of mail that needed attention.

I figured my hands-free telephone headset would come in handy, so I put it on my head. I dialed the first number on my list of calls and headed to the kitchen.

I popped a chicken into the oven while I instructed my insurance agent to add my new car to my policy. I set the oven to roast and headed back to my office.

Then I called the DMV to find out what forms to file when I sold my car. I waited while the recording told me to hold on. While I listened to the DMV's Muzak tunes, I turned on my computer and picked up my e-mail.

I read my new messages, responded to a few of them and shut off the computer. As I listened to the DMV's recorded message about forms, I jotted down the information I needed. Great! A few more to-do's out of the way.

I adjusted my headset and hit the play button on my message machine. I listened to the calls that had come in earlier while I'd been writing. While I listened, I grabbed the stack of mail from my in-basket, picked up the letter opener and got to work.

I was about ready to tear into the first envelope when I stopped. I set the mail down and put the brakes on. I hung up the phone, took off my headset and placed it on my desk.

I took a deep breath.

I realized just then that I'd been cruising through the day in the fast lane.

I took another deep breath and decided to change lanes.

I looked at my watch. I had one hour until my client called.

I carried the stack of mail out of my office, stopped in the kitchen for a glass of mineral water and headed into the family room. I rummaged through a basket of videotapes and grabbed a few-years-old tape of the Rosie O'Donnell show I'd never made time to watch. I popped the tape into the VCR, kicked back and collapsed onto the sofa.

As the tape played, I began to sort through the mile-high stack of mail. From my reclined position, I could hear Rosie O'Donnell's show more than I could see it.

I tossed several junk-mail flyers in a recycle pile and heard Rosie say she'd be right back with her next guest.

I picked up the remote, fast-forwarded through the commercial for quilted bathroom-tissue and rejoined Rosie. I half-heard her greet her guest as I tore through another envelope.

Then I heard Rosie say to her guest, "Can you do multi-tasking? Are you good at it?"

I sat upright on the couch.

"No, I can't...and I'm not," the guest said.

I leaned forward.

Rosie said she was great at multi-tasking. She revealed that she could watch TV, knit, and read a book at the same time. And she seemed ecstatic about this fact.

I put down the envelope I was holding and picked up the remote. I hit the PAUSE button.

"Uh-oh," I said aloud, gulped, and turned off the TV. I was busted—caught speeding in my life by my own inner patrol-officer.

I walked back to my office, placed the remaining mail on my desk, picked up my client files and took the telephone handset with me as I went outside to the backyard.

I sat in a cushioned patio-chair and put my feet up on a footstool. Again I took a deep breath. This time I looked around at my garden.

I noticed the leaves of the maple tree had begun to turn red and orange. I noticed my shoulders were tight so I began to rub them. I noticed the air was crisp and the sun was warm.

When the handset rang, I gave my full attention to my client. It was a delicious half hour.

Later that evening, after my writing group left, I spent some time writing in my journal.

I think we were put on this earth to enjoy the garden of life—to savor each task before us as if it were a smooth butterscotch candy. And whether that task is putting a Band-Aid on your kid's first skinned knee, making a call to the DMV, or even dealing with your own grief and sorrow, there is only one way to taste the sweetness of butterscotch as it melts on your tongue—you have to do it one piece of butterscotch candy at a time. No multi-tasking allowed.

I put my pen down.

I knew then, that if Rosie O'Donnell were ever to ask me if I could multi-task, my answer would be, "Why would I want to?"

INQUIRIES:

- **If you said "no" to multi-tasking, even once today, what would open up for you?**
- **What small things are the "butterscotch candy of life" for you?**
- **What would it be like to savor even the tough times?**

I WOULD HAVE STOPPED ANYWAY

While driving to my dentist's office in Albany, I decided to break from my usual scenic-route and go directly through town—for the sake of variety and to help save myself some time. Though I wasn't late, I didn't want to be...so the shortcut held appeal.

Heading down Solano Avenue, for the first time in ages, I *did* take time to notice that the once-tired area had undergone some big changes.

Baskets of flowers hung on the once rusty and now painted streetlamps. The City must have repaved the street, I thought—it's dark-black and spotless—and it's also much wider than it used to be. Continuing on my way, I glanced at the updated storefronts on both sides of the street—they were charming with their new green awnings. Shoppers filed in and out of each one. The area had become awake and alive with life.

I checked the clock on my dashboard, noted I was making good time, and resumed my observations of the refreshed neighborhood—but the opportunities to do so came from a few more Stop Signs than I'd remembered, and not from any purposeful dawdling.

While stopped at one intersection, I noticed that even the old Chinese produce market, which I remembered as being dark and quiet most days, looked brighter and busier—the owners had moved bins and carts of fresh produce out to the sidewalk, inviting passersby to pinch a melon or smell an orange. The changes made me smile as I drove along.

The sweetest change I discovered was the addition of the

senior citizen Crossing Guards who were stationed at each street corner. Eyes alert and narrowed in concentration, they watched for pedestrians who needed to traverse the new cobblestone crosswalks. The seniors sported official Crossing Guard uniforms—white shoulder harnesses, whistles that hung on lanyard necklaces, white hats with sun visors—and they held large, wooden Stop Signs.

But after a number of Crossing-Guard-enforced stops, my delight began to wear off—my smile faded and my impatience grew—I wondered just how many *more* times I was going to be delayed. Maybe this change *isn't* so sweet, I thought. Between sighs, I found I had nothing to do at each stop but to note the Crossing-Guard safety routine:

There were three whistles involved in the ritual. The first came as the Crossing Guard stepped into the crosswalk with the standard-issue Stop Sign. A quick motion to the waiting pedestrians told them to cross the street. The second whistle informed the drivers that the pedestrians had arrived safely and, as the Guard returned to the sidewalk, the third toot told us it was safe to go.

The realization that I'd memorized the routine was a rude reminder that I'd waited for pedestrians at each and every blasted crosswalk I'd come to so far. My previously pleasant, though unplanned, sightseeing experience had disappeared behind a cloud of frustration. I fumed as I looked at the time again; I was now "almost late" for my dental appointment.

I'd become oblivious to the individuals who served as Crossing Guards—I saw only uniforms and Stop Signs—however, I couldn't help but notice the woman who was stationed at the next crosswalk.

She must have been 90 years old if she was a day. But 90 or not, she had a job to do. A gaggle of children wanted to cross the street and with the first shrill blast of her whistle she was damn well going to stop traffic to be sure they could.

With that same whistle blast, I somehow remembered to take a deep breath, notice I was causing myself a lot of grief by fretting about the time, and decided to just sit back and appreciate the scene before me.

Slight, stooped, and frail-looking, the Crossing Guard hoisted her wooden Stop Sign—which had to be heavier than she was—and carried it with her as she took slow steps away from the sidewalk and onto the cobblestones; the kids followed behind.

I watched—with almost bated-breath—wondering whether the woman herself would make a safe crossing.

She reached the midway point of the street and planted herself right in front of my car. With a scowl on her face, born of responsibility and determination, she managed to wave the Stop Sign at me to be sure I knew she meant business. Then she held the sign out in front of her, arms as stiff as rods. The children crossed, she blew her whistle again, and when she arrived back at the sidewalk, she gave the third tweet.

By the time I left her station, I realized I'd stopped more than just my *car* at that intersection. I shook my head in amazement. Madam Crossing Guard, I thought, I would have stopped the car anyway—you didn't even need the sign—but watching you do your work in the world helped me remember to take a breath, slow myself down, and notice the "gotta-get-there" way I'd been making myself miserable. Stopping for you was my pleasure.

INQUIRIES:

- **What is it for you to be as patient with yourself as you would be with a 90-year-old?**
- **What would it be like to know that your work in the world is sacred?**
- **What is it to take in some of your own sweetness?**

BILLBOARD MANIA

Driving along a Bay Area freeway almost five years ago, I noticed an eye-catching billboard that advertised Macintosh's then-latest laptop computer. An enlarged photograph of the white, 2001 iBook covered fifty percent of the sign. The other half was consumed by four words that disturbed me: "Your Life. To Go®."

My mouth agape, I began an entire inner dialogue about the notion of "To Go" as society's new religion...and how I would *not* become a member. I could feel my brow wrinkle as my silent rant continued. You can order almost *anything* "to go," I thought—from take-out-food to digital photos and cups of drive-through coffee—and now your *life*?

It seemed to me that the designers of the ad campaign were telling me that a life "to go" had value—that living a fast-paced life was a fact of life and they had a tool to help me keep up. "Well," I said to the phantom designers, "the only thing *I'll* take 'to go' is the next exit!"

I called my friend, Peller, when I got home. As we each assembled ingredients for supper, we talked about the implications of the billboard message.

"Is it such a virtue to be able to do just about anything on the run?" I said.

I could hear her chopping vegetables. "No, it's not," she said. "And God forbid my computer should become my *life*...let alone, *to go*."

"No kidding. You know, I'll admit I use my laptop every day—

which, just in case you don't remember, happens to be a Mac—and I do own a Palm Pilot and make critical calls on my cell phone every now and then, but overall...I'm committed to staying in the *slow* lane of life these days. I don't want my life "to go."

"Me, neither," Peller said.

We talked about the growing trend of "healthy" fast-food and how it misses the mark—it's still of the "to go" mentality and it doesn't teach us to stay put while we eat—even though it looks like it's better for us.

We affirmed how glad we were that we'd made time for our friendship over the past nineteen years—even in the midst of a "to go" culture that finds little time for human contact—and how glad we were that were taking time for a slow-paced call.

"Talk to you soon," Peller said at the end of our chat.

"Bye," I said, thankful the billboard had been such a clear reminder of my own values.

Days later, we laughed that we'd each returned to our tasks of preparing slow food that had no take-out ingredients.

INQUIRIES:

- **If you had a container labeled "*To Stay*," what would you put inside?**
- **What would your personal billboard say...the one that describes your life values?**

HUMMINGBIRDS

We moved into our new house in the spring. The unpacking seemed endless. One day that first week, I took a break from all the cardboard boxes and decided to go outside. There wasn't much to our unlandscaped property yet, but I needed some fresh air.

When I got out to the back yard, I discovered a surprise—two iridescent green and fuchsia hummingbirds flying overhead. I was delighted. I hadn't seen any hummingbirds in the yard of our old house in all the years we lived there.

The hummingbirds were headed for our neighbor's bottlebrush bushes, which grew up and over our back fence. I could see the shimmering birds drink from the bushes' red flowers.

I had always been amazed that hummingbirds could keep their busy wing-action going while they gathered nectar. These two little treasures rekindled my amazement. Talk about multi-tasking. I guess we all do what it takes to get our needs met, I thought. On that note, I stretched my arms, grabbed a few deep breaths of fresh air and went back inside to unpack more boxes.

The spring season passed but my move-in activities and busy pace did not.

As I write this, it is now near the end of our first summer in our new house. The red bottlebrush blooms have faded and dropped. They didn't get much hummingbird action the last few months—at least none that I'd found time to notice.

Until this morning.

I sat out back to take a break from my writing. I just sat. For an hour. The stillness felt delicious. I wasn't checking out the clouds, or looking for the neighborhood squirrels, or noticing things that I could write about. I just sat. It was bliss.

After a while, I sensed there was something near our back fence. Without thinking, I turned my head toward the bottlebrush bushes. There sat a hummingbird.

She was perched on a leafy branch now devoid of red flowers. Her wings weren't humming. She wasn't moving. She was sitting still. I bet, if I had been close enough, I could have heard her breathing...or heard her heart beating. Or maybe she could have heard mine.

We were both at complete rest—off duty. No nectar to gather, no soaring heights to attain to scope out worthy targets, no fast dives down to land in a blossom.

Just resting.

It seems I discover delightful surprises in our back yard with each season we live here...if I just take the time.

INQUIRIES:

- **As you sip the nectar of this story, what is the rhythm of your heartbeat?**
- **What becomes available to you when you rest?**

WAITING FOR MYSELF

This morning I completed some routine paperwork that I wanted to send to my accountant. After I addressed and stamped the envelope, I grabbed my keys, locked the front door, and headed for my car. I needed to go to the post office.

Halfway down the front walk I stopped. There was no hurry. The accountant didn't need the stuff right away, so why was I rushing to the post office? I could put the envelope in our mailbox, with the flag up, and let the mail carrier pick it up.

But I was compelled to go to the post office, even though it was ninety-two degrees outside—at eleven o'clock in the morning—and heat aggravates my physical symptoms.

Why don't I wait 'til it's cooler, I asked myself as I put my keys into the ignition. I drove down the street, chuckling at the absurdity of this trip. I had better things to do...but on I went.

I mailed my letter and headed home. At the intersection around the corner from my house, I glanced in all four directions to check for cars. The roads were clear. On I drove. But my brain stayed behind.

Something had registered in my peripheral vision. In the brief moment that I'd glanced to the left of the intersection, I saw something unusual. Something that wasn't right. Something that caused me enough concern to make a u-turn and drive back to the side street I'd just passed. As I neared the street, I discovered what I'd seen. Or rather whom I'd seen.

An old man stood on the sidewalk, five feet from the corner. He was hunched over, freeze-framed in the hot summer sun, staring down at the sidewalk and clutching a small, brown-paper bag. The man wore a down-filled winter jacket.

A deep part of me knew something was wrong with this picture. Why wasn't he moving? Why was this frail looking man standing outside without a companion to help him, on a day when the sun could bake a pie?

I pulled up alongside the man and rolled down the passenger window. "Are you okay? Do you need help?"

Without moving from his spot, and without turning his head to look at me, he answered. "Yes. As a matter of fact, if you could give me a lift to my driveway it would be nice." His voice was as calm as bath water.

I leaned over, opened the passenger door and said, "No problem. Come...get in and I'll take you to your house."

He continued to stand there.

I wasn't sure what he needed. "Would you like some help getting into the car?"

"No, I'll just be a moment."

And so I waited.

He was silent.

My waiting continued for several minutes. I noticed my own discomfort with the silence. "I have a cane in the car. Do you want to use it?" I said.

"No, thank you," the man said. "I just need to wait for my legs to move. I've got a chronic thing with my middle ear. It makes my legs unsteady and slow. It's usually not this bad. But I'll get there," he told me.

For a moment I was dumbfounded. This man had not moved

one inch since I'd first noticed him. But I recognized the reason: He was waiting for the signals to travel from his brain to his feet. And I understood. I had similar challenges in my own body.

At that moment, I knew the only thing this man needed from me was to wait.

And so I did.

I sat with the car door open and I heard myself say to him, "Take your time. I'm in no rush."

I realized that I was in it for whatever time it took him to move. And I found the waiting to be a quiet honor.

A couple of minutes passed and then he made a few quick shuffles to the car. Two or three minutes more and he grabbed the door to get in.

He took a long, deep breath and said, "May I set this parcel down?" He held the small, brown-paper bag in his outstretched hand.

I placed the bag between us and turned up the air conditioner. "There. Now, where do you live? Give me the directions and we're off," I said.

"That house right there," he said, pointing across the street.

I put the gar in gear and drove him fifty feet to his home.

"Let me help you to your front door," I said.

"No, thank you, dear. I'll make my own way to the front door. I just need you to wait for me, while I wait for myself, to get out of the car."

And so we sat for a few air-conditioned minutes.

When he was ready, he opened the door. A blast of hot air hit us as he awaited his next impulse to move. He waited another minute. Then he lifted one foot out of the car.

We waited.

"My feet," he said, "are like two girls dancing—neither one can decide who wants to take the lead." He laughed, despite the sweat beading up on his brow, despite the intense heat and the effort of his ordeal.

While we waited for his muscles to move again, he pointed to the paper sack and said, "I had to get to the drug store to get my medicine."

"Did you walk all that way?" I was now in further disbelief than I'd been. The nearest drug store had to be at least two miles.

"No, I took the bus from the corner," he said. "But I left early today, before the sun was too hot."

He made a series of quick movements. "Oh. I'm out," he said, now standing beside the car. "Will you hand me my bag of medicines?"

I gave him the brown bag. "Are you sure you don't want help to the door?"

"Yes, I'm sure. Thank you, dear. You did enough."

I waited as he leaned on the hood of the car. I waited for him as he made his way down the walkway toward his front door. As he did, I thought, Thank you, sir, for reminding me to wait for myself. I don't know your name, but my heart knows your heart. May you be well.

I pulled away with a sense of amazement. This man was so accepting of his slowness. I bet he would have waited all day on the hot sidewalk for his own pace to begin.

I could use his lesson. My own slow pace often frustrated me.

It wouldn't hurt me at all to practice waiting for myself—and to practice waiting with quiet honor.

Who knew that a trip to the post office would hold such value?

INQUIRIES:

- **Where do you wait for yourself?**
- **What unexpected lessons have you learned when you have given to others?**
- **Where in your life do you want to cultivate a sense of patience with yourself?**

SACRED ATTITUDE FOUR:
DO LESS

Speak without words, work without doing
Few realize how much how little will do.

—Lao Tsu

Besides the noble art of getting things done, there is the noble art of leaving things undone. The wisdom of life consists in the elimination of nonessentials.

—Lin Yutang

A wind that continually changes direction...even a very powerful one, has no real effect. Enduring accomplishments are won through gentle but ceaseless penetration, like that of a soft wind blowing steadily in the same direction.

—Brian Browne Walker, *The I Ching*

The fourth Sacred Attitude, *Do Less*, comes from a guiding principle in Traditional Chinese Medicine (TCM) called the "Law of Least Action."

The "Law of Least Action" instructs the acupuncturist, as well as others, to be mindful when expending energy and to know the right moment to do only what is necessary.

The "Law of Least Action" is the antithesis of the pervasive "Do More" attitude in our culture that tells us to push ahead, multi-task, and borrow from tomorrow's energy reserves just like it tells us to borrow with our credit cards.

In the modern world, we have come to believe that if a little action is good, then more action is better.

Microsoft's *Office 2005 Dictionary* shows us—in black and white—the effects of the "Do More" attitude:

Do: v - to wear somebody out

More: adv pron - with greater frequency or intensity

Another Way

The "Law of Least Action" shows us that there is another way to live. We can embrace this way when we embrace the Sacred Attitude, *Do Less*.

In his book, *365 Tao*, author Deng Ming-Dao includes a passage that's the best illustration of the *Do Less* attitude and the "Law of Least Action" that I have ever read:

> *...There is a fable about a king who was watching his butcher. He was amazed that the man could dismember a whole ox without much effort and without dulling his knife. Seeking to*

learn, the king questioned his servant, who said that his secret was to insert his knife only in the spaces between muscles, thus parting the body along its natural lines. In this way, where an ordinary butcher had to grind his blade daily, he only had to sharpen his knife once a year....

—Deng Ming-Dao, *365 Tao*

Acupuncturists insert their fine needles into the fewest points possible to move stuck energy and bring about balance in the body. In a similar way, the *Do Less* attitude asks us to *be the needle* in our own lives...to conserve our energy and look for the least action needed.

Just as the discipline of making consistent financial investments helps us acquire wealth, the on-going practice of the *Do Less* attitude can lead to an abundance of riches in our lives.

The essays in this section highlight the power of the *Do Less* attitude...the power of eliminating unnecessary energy-expenditures and bringing careful attention and awareness to the actions we take.

THE TAO OF IMPINGEMENT

I was forty-something and I was stuck. Try as I might I couldn't make anything new happen in several key areas of my life. When I tried, I kept hitting roadblocks—in my career, my Yoga practice, and my writing.

My intellectual mind knew the life lesson before me—"Don't push things." But I wasn't a very good student.

Until I pushed too far.

One summer day, I stayed in the pool—swimming laps—longer than I'd intended. My usual swim was a half-mile. On that day, I decided to go all out and swim an entire mile. I'd never done that before. I hadn't trained for it, either. When I finished, I dragged myself out of the pool. I was tired—but so what? The joy of stretching my limits filled me. Thank God, I thought at the time. At least I made progress somewhere in my life.

A week later, my body had a different story to tell. My right shoulder wouldn't move. My marathon swim wasn't progress after all. I had pushed too far, too fast, and pinched a nerve in my shoulder.

I read a medical article in my chiropractor's office and learned that the medical term for my shoulder condition was "impingement"—which meant that something was getting in the way of smooth-flowing nerve conduction. I further translated the medical jargon to mean this: if you placed a dam of boulders across a rushing river that was used to generate power, people downstream would be eating by candlelight. Well, downstream from my impinged shoulder, my fingers couldn't move well enough to write.

I finished reading the medical article and tossed it to the side. Great—impingement in my shoulder, impingement in my life. I wondered if I could take a simple truckload of dynamite to all the rock-like obstacles in my life, including my shoulder, and blast my way clear.

But my chiropractor, Dr. Craig, suggested a different tactic for handling my shoulder's impingement problem. He told me, "The strategy is this: you begin where you are. If there is impingement, there is impingement. Just work with it."

"Okay," I said. "How?"

He explained the process and we began.

The first week, I was to take it easy. "Use ice and heat to reduce swelling," he said, "and get lots of rest." I wasn't supposed to move my shoulder. I wasn't even supposed to *attempt* to move my shoulder. Excruciating pain and immobility helped me go along with the plan.

The following week, Dr. Craig said, "Show me the extent of the movement you now have in your shoulder."

"Right," I said. "I can tell you. There isn't any."

But he urged me to try a technique for moving my shoulder that he said would be gentle. So I sat in a chair, bent over toward the floor, extended my arm straight down to my feet and let my arm hang down. No problem so far.

"Now use your arm like a pendulum," he said. "Make circular arm movements from that position, within the range that you're able. However small."

I held my arm like a pendulum and made 2-inch circles. I

winced with pain.

"Well, that face tells me you went too far," Dr. Craig noted. "Take it down to a smaller circle. No bigger than a dime this week. I want you to work within your limits."

"Working within my limits has not been my strong suit," I said.

"Until today," my chiropractor said. "Change your attitude. This week you'll get to see the power of small movements. Here's what you'll practice: make the small circles that you can, back off when you feel a twinge, find your limit and stay there."

I went home and practiced each day. I found it frustrating. I wanted to reach farther—to make larger circles. But I remembered there'd be a payoff if I stayed within my limits and so I kept to my dime-sized circles.

Back in Dr. Craig's office the next week, I told him of my daily arm-circle practice. "But I'm still sore," I said. "I still feel the same twinge of pain in my shoulder when I move it."

"Show me."

I bent down and began my arm circles.

"At what point do you feel the twinge?" he asked.

I moved my arm and showed him the place where my arm started to hurt.

"Well, Erica, of course it still hurts you when you move to your limit. That's how you know it's your limit. When you're at home, I want you stop *before* the extent of your limit. But look at your progress. Do you see how your circles are now more than double the size that they were a week ago?"

Oops. I was looking in the wrong place for progress. I was looking for an immediate and total absence of the pain. I forgot to notice the circles had expanded to the size of a baseball and the pain didn't kick in until my new limit.

As I got into my car to go home and practice my next week's circles, I glanced at the cover of the book I'd left on the passenger's seat. It showed a picture of the Grand Canyon.

Huh. What a metaphor for all I was learning. Water created that entire canyon. Over time. Bit by bit. The water didn't insist upon an immediate result. It just kept moving in one direction.

I began to think of my daily arm-circle practice as the "Tao of Impingement." I realized that I could apply this philosophy to my entire life. For example, I could look at my writing and my Yoga practice and notice any impingement of my creative or physical energy flow. Then I could apply the same principle that I was learning from my shoulder rehabilitation process. I could stay within my limits and see where that took me.

And so I began to apply the "Tao of Impingement" principles to my writing, my career, and my Yoga practice, in addition to my shoulder. With each little movement, focused in the direction I wanted to go, I noticed something remarkable. My limits began to expand. The creative energy was flowing again.

And I did not touch anything that even resembled dynamite.

INQUIRIES:

- **Where in your life are you tempted to use "dynamite"?**
- **In your most stuck place, where are small actions possible?**

THE "N" EXERCISE

I sat in the leather dental chair and thumbed through *People* magazine. I'd just started reading an article on Brad Pitt when my hygienist, Pam, came in.

"No more juicy reading for you today, honey. Let's clean your teeth." She fastened a green paper bib around my neck. "How are your teeth and gums? Anything new I should know about?"

"Things have been fine," I told her. And then I remembered a new development. "Except for one thing. When I bite down and close my mouth, I can move my jaw forward and back even though my teeth are together and I'm still biting down. Does this mean my teeth are shifting? After years of orthodontia as a kid, I hate to think I have to go through that again."

Pam smiled. "Erica, dear, you're experiencing Bruxism."

"What's that?"

"Grinding your teeth."

"Me? I don't grind my teeth," I said. "Don't people do that at night? Wouldn't Steve have noticed?"

"Well, *some* people grind their teeth at night," Pam said as she tilted my head back and turned on her dental lamp. "Others grind their teeth during the day. And many of us clench our teeth and don't even realize it. Jaws are a place where many people hold tension. When you're moving your jaw back and forth during the day, checking and changing your bite, you're grinding your teeth. I'll bet you're stressed—have you been feeling tense?"

"Not really," I said, as she put a suction hose in my mouth.

As Pam continued to clean my teeth, I mulled over what she'd just asked me. Come to think of it, a number of stress-factors *had* entered my life recently—a new house, an increased client load, a writing deadline—and they contributed to my having a year's worth of tasks on my daily "to do" lists. On top of it all, swimming—my usual avenue for tension-release—was presently unavailable to me; it had been so for a few months, while my strained shoulder healed from an over-aggressive swim.

The more I thought about my current pace and level of stress, the more I realized my hygienist's guess about my stress-level was right on the money.

Pam finished up, unfastened my bib and turned to write some notes in my file. As I waited for her, I noticed I was grinding my teeth. Huh. Until that moment, I hadn't realized I'd developed such a definitive habit.

"Okay, Pam. Help me out here. For years, I've been doing Yoga and Tai Chi for *overall* relaxation. But is there anything specific I can do that will help me stop grinding my teeth?"

She put down her notes and turned to me. "Well," she said, "sometimes we give patients a night guard. It looks like a football player's mouth guard. But I don't think you need one. There's a simpler tool you could try. It's called the 'N' exercise."

Pam pushed the button on the chair and tilted me upright. She said, "Say the letter 'N.'"

"'N'. Now what?"

"There is no 'now what?'" Pam said. "The exercise is about finding a resting spot for your jaw and tongue. Say 'N' again. But this time, stop after your tongue comes down from the roof of your mouth. Notice how your jaws stay apart and relaxed. Stay in that position. Even when your lips are closed, try to keep your jaws a slight bit apart. Just resting."

Oh. Just resting.

I let my mind wander while Pam finished her notes. She'd told me that the "N" exercise was a place to rest. I had jumped right in wondering what else to do, thinking that there had to be *more* to the exercise than saying "N." But nothing else was required.

The "N" exercise is like the Free Parking space in the Monopoly game, I mused. Every space on the Monopoly board, except for Free Parking, directs players who land there to make, or consider making, a financial transaction—a purchase, a payment for a fine, or a rent payment to another player. Not so with the Free Parking space. As I remember it, the official rulebook of the game says that Free Parking is meant as a space where you don't have to make any financial transactions. You land there and you rest. But there's been a grassroots-change over the last twenty years in the way people play Monopoly.

Somewhere along the line, people got bored with just resting on the Free Parking space. In Monopoly games played across America, players now designate the center of the game board as a place to put cash fines and penalties that once went to the bank. Any player landing on the Free Parking space now gets all the money that has accumulated in the center of the board. Like our busy lives, even the Free Parking space is filled with activity—it's no longer a place for just resting.

As Pam took my bib off, I brought my mind back to the dental office. She declared my mouth to be in great shape, and sent me off saying "N."

When I got home, Steve asked about my day. I rattled off the list of things I'd done and places I'd gone, ending with mention of my dental visit.

"Oh, how was that?" he said.

"Great," I explained. "Pam taught me how to say 'N.'"

"What?"

I showed him the "N" exercise. "After you say 'N,' you let your jaw rest." He tried it.

"Cool," he said. "I don't grind my teeth but I sure must have the 'I need to learn to rest' sign emblazed on my forehead today—I've been trying to do way too much. Maybe if I can teach my jaw to do less, the rest of me will follow."

We both headed down the hallway saying "N."

I'm always amazed at the power of simple things. I'm more amazed when I've been struggling with something and a simpler way is right underneath my nose. Or my tongue, as the case may be.

NO INQUIRIES TODAY...FREE PARKING

- **Try the "N" exercise.**

PURSUING & ALLOWING

To every thing there is a season,
and a time to every purpose under the heaven:
A time to be born, and a time to die;
a time to plant, and a time to pluck up that which is planted;
A time to kill, and a time to heal;
a time to break down, and a time to build up;
A time to weep, and a time to laugh;
a time to mourn, and a time to dance;
A time to cast away stones, and a time to gather stones together;
a time to embrace, and a time to refrain from embracing;
A time to get, and a time to lose;
a time to keep, and a time to cast away;
A time to rend, and a time to sow;
a time to keep silence, and a time to speak;
A time to love, and a time to hate;
a time of war, and a time of peace.

—Ecclesiastes 3:1-8

My nutritionist, Dr. Jack, plays an important role on my health care team. He provides me with nutritional advice that is brilliant. He also offers me life-changing perspectives that are invaluable. One day, last fall, I had an appointment with him that contained both.

For the first half-hour of my appointment, we reviewed my current nutritional supplements and discussed some modifications to the plan. After that, I brought up something I'd been waiting to discuss with him for weeks.

"There's a physical therapy technique I'd like to talk to you about," I said. "I'd like to know what you think." Since Dr. Jack was also a chiropractor, I knew his opinion would be a great addition to what I'd discovered so far.

"Okay. What's the technique?" he said.

I pulled a glossy tri-fold brochure out of my purse. "It's all in here," I said, handing him the material. "Have you heard of this method?"

He held the brochure and put on his reading glasses. "Let's see," he said, raising one eyebrow. He inspected the cover and read the first page. "Hmm. No, Erica, I haven't heard of this exact approach," he said. "But at first glance, the technique looks like it's based on biofeedback...and that's something I *do* know about. But before I say more, give me a minute and let me look at the details."

I waited in anticipation while Dr. Jack combed the material. As soon as he finished, he re-folded the brochure and put his reading glasses back in his shirt pocket.

I couldn't wait another minute. "Well, any thoughts?"

"Several," he said. "First of all, using biofeedback can be a great way for people who overtax their muscles to learn to relax them—"

"Yes!" I said, interrupting him in my excitement. "And since I exert so much muscle effort when I walk, I thought it might help me learn a way to make my gait more efficient."

"Biofeedback *can* help that way," Dr. Jack said. "And over time, you would probably learn how to activate only the muscles needed for walking, while turning off the muscles that you don't need—you wouldn't have to work so hard. But—"

"I know the sessions are twice a week for twelve weeks, but I think I could fit them into my schedule," I said without taking a breath, "especially since the physical therapist is right here in the Bay Area. So, do you think it's a good thing for me to add to my health routine?"

Dr. Jack stayed quiet for a very long moment. Then he said, "I sense it's a good thing. But let me also say this: there is *pursuing* and then there is *allowing*. I think you do plenty of pursuing, Erica."

"Oh."

"Ponder that idea," Dr. Jack said, "and the next time we meet, we can talk about this some more." He handed the brochure back to me and hugged me goodbye.

I left the office, thinking about Dr. Jack's words. He had provided another life-changing perspective. He didn't say, "This physical therapy regime will not be good for you...don't do it." Nor did he say, "Go do it." He'd given me a simple reminder—a reminder that my tendency in life was to *pursue* things. And I had been a damn good pursuer. But until that moment, I hadn't given much thought to the notion of *allowing*.

True to form, I went home to pursue one more thing. I looked up the word "pursue" in *Webster's Dictionary*. What I found mirrored Dr. Jack's emphasis:

pursue: to follow in order to over-take

Then I looked up the word "allow" and read an eye-opener:

allow: agree to the truth of

Ahh.

Right then, I began to consider what my life would be like if I were to *allow* healing—if I "agreed to the truth of" my healing. Even the possibility seemed to open more space.

I took Dr. Jack's words to heart. I realized that, in the healing and health arena, it would be a good idea for me to learn to balance the *pursuing* I do by *allowing* healing to take place. This became more than just a good idea.

As the months went by, I learned to stop, take a few deep breaths and discern whether it was time to *pursue* something on my health journey—find a new practitioner, a new modality or regime—or whether it was time to *allow*. The discernment got easier over time. I came to enjoy the allowing.

Recently, I had a short phone conversation with Dr. Jack about the notion of *pursuing* and *allowing*.

"I wrote a poem about *allowing*, Dr. Jack. It's going to go in the book I'm writing—along with an essay on the subject. Is there anything more you think I should add to the pot about *allowing*—or *pursuing*?"

"Well, why not emphasize the importance of balance—of taking an 'and' sort of an approach to applying these ideas in life, rather than an 'or' approach?"

"Thanks for the reminder," I said.

We ended our call and I ended my *pursuit* of more information. Then I sat and *allowed* the rest of this essay to write it itself:

In Western culture, we seem to do a pretty good job with *pursuing*. But life wasn't meant to be one-sided. Nature shows us by example that we need to balance our time spent *pursuing*, with time spent *allowing*.

Spring and summer are the earth's time for blooming and for increased movement. Time for more action. Time for *pursuing*. But new growth, blossoms and action aren't the end of nature's story.

Fall and winter are the earth's time for slowing down and being still. Time for resting. Time for *allowing*. But stillness, falling leaves and hibernation are also not the only piece of nature's puzzle.

No season exists without the other. No season is a more admirable season than the other. We need them all. In their own time.

Just like nature, we need to create a balance of "seasons" within the days, weeks, months, and years of our lives. Time for "pursuing" and time for "allowing."

It is my time to allow.

Agreeing to the Truth...

Allow
Let it be
Receive
Take it in
Fill up
Allow that soft magnificent temple of your body
to dance its own dance
to find its own rhythm
to do what it knows how to do
to heal in its own time

Sing
Dance
Sleep
Paint
Work
Eat
Write
or rush to the office to close a deal
or swim a mile.
just
do so
in your
own time
Allow

—ERK

INQUIRIES:

- **Where in your life is there more room for allowing?**
- **What is possible when you allow?**
- **What do you need to pursue now?**

FISHING

I met my friend, Anna, for lunch last Tuesday. We'd gone to nutrition school together years ago. Although I'm a coach now and Anna is a nutritionist, we often like to share business ideas.

"Hey, Erica," Anna said between bites of her chicken salad. "Do you want to buy advertising space in my professional association's newsletter? Your coaching services could really serve the nutrition members well."

I hadn't advertised before—other than my website—but I heard myself say, "Good idea. I'll buy a half-page."

"Great."

We settled the deal, finished lunch and said our goodbyes. I went home to draw up plans for an ad.

While I worked on the copy, I began to think of all the other places I could advertise my coaching practice. I was excited. Within short order, I came up with a list of ten more publications for my ad, including one newsletter that would reach the hundreds of health care practitioners who make up a large sector of my target audience.

As the day continued, so did my mental activity. By late afternoon, I had expanded my list to twenty-five places to advertise, including radio spots and major newspapers.

At dinner, I told my husband about my day. "Honey, my coaching practice is going to expand in a big way now. When I place the ad in Anna's newsletter and advertise in all of the other places I've identified, I'll reach hundreds—maybe thousands—of potential clients."

Steve was quiet for a moment.

Then he said, "The ad in Anna's newsletter sounds like a good match for you. Congratulations." He took a bite of salmon, chewed, swallowed and said, "Do you think you need to advertise beyond that? I mean you seem to be happy with the number of clients you get from word-of-mouth and your website. A few more from Anna's association would be cool, but I thought think you didn't want a huge business—that you wanted to keep things small and intimate."

I stopped eating. My fork froze in mid-air. My mouth hung wide open. I took a deep breath. Steve had just reminded me of my personal agenda to have a coaching practice of quality not quantity.

"Oh," I said.

Then I took another bite of salmon, deep in thought.

We finished eating in a pregnant silence. When we'd cleared the table, cleaned the kitchen and dried the last pot, I said, "I think I'll go work in my office for a while. I've still got books to put on my new bookshelves." I gave Steve a quick kiss and headed down the hallway, all the while thinking about his comment.

In my office, I glanced at the list of advertising options I'd created throughout the day. I shrugged and went to my bookshelves.

As I moved books and magazines from my old bookshelf onto my new one, I pondered the question, "What is enough?"

The question filled my mind as I continued to fill my new shelves. But only for a while.

While hefting a stack of worn magazines I'd been saving, I got distracted from my pondering. I read the date on the top issue and set the stack down. Could it be? The issues went back almost eight years. I pulled one of the oldest from the pile.

Did I need to keep it? I flipped through the pages of the Traditional Acupuncture Institute's *Quintessence* magazine and found my attention resting on the following fable:

Enough Fish For The Day

The rich industrialist was horrified to find the fisherman lying lazily beside his boat, smoking a pipe. "Why aren't you out fishing?" asked the industrialist.

"Because I have caught enough fish for the day," said the fisherman.

"Why don't you catch some more?"

"What would I do with them?"

"You could earn more money," said the industrialist. "With that you could have a motor fixed to your boat to go into deeper waters and catch more fish. Then you would make enough money to buy nylon nets. The nets would bring you more fish and more money. Soon you would have enough money to own two boats, maybe even a fleet of boats. Then you would be a rich man like me."

"What would I do then?"

"Then you could really enjoy life."

"What do you think I am doing right now?"

—*Quintessence*, Winter, 1994

For the second time that evening, my mouth hung open. I put the magazine down, walked to my desk and turned on my computer.

In fifteen minutes I finished writing the ad for Anna's newsletter, printed it, sealed it in an envelope and addressed it. Then I picked up my list of twenty-five more advertising options, ripped it in half and went back to sorting books.

Thanks to Steve's reminder, I realized I'd caught enough fish for the day.

INQUIRIES:

- **What is enough?**
- **What excess activities do you want to shed?**
- **What does it mean to enjoy what you have?**

TAKING THE TIME

One Friday morning, while assembling the material that would go into this book, I thumbed through the stack of essays for the section then called "The Law of Least Action." I wondered if I'd written enough to make my point.

The Law of Least Action is a difficult concept to illustrate, I thought. Maybe I need to write a few more essays on the subject. I began to make a list of ideas.

Ten minutes later I glanced at my watch. Well, no time to finish this now, I warned myself. I'm late for my writing get-together with Bonnie. I put down the essays, grabbed the list and headed out the door.

I drove to Tacker's Café to join up with my friend and writing cohort, Bonnie. On Fridays we do "writing practice" and share writing ideas. We also talk shop.

Along the way, I decided what I wanted to talk to Bonnie about that day. As a retired psychotherapist, and now a writer, Bonnie listens with care and knows our craft well. Did she think I had enough essays for the "Law of Least Action" section? Did I need a few more stories to convey my message? I'd also show her my list of ideas for more content and see what she thought.

I arrived at Tacker's and found Bonnie already sitting at our favorite corner booth, working on a bagel. I ordered myself a Chai Tea and sat across from her.

"Get any good writing done this week?" I said.

Bonnie grinned. "Yes. And I also attended a great lecture at our local bookstore. I have to tell you about it before we start writing."

"Fine by me," I said, setting my writing notebook and pen off to one side. "But don't let me forget...I've got a burning question for you about my book when you finish the story."

"Great. It's not a long story, anyway. But I've been saving it for you 'til we met today."

"Okay, go for it. I'll just work on this cup of tea." I loved hearing Bonnie talk about a good writing lecture.

"Well, Thursday night, Thom Steinbeck, John Steinbeck's son, was a guest at the bookstore," Bonnie said. "His presentation was so inspiring I wanted to run home and write."

"Hmm," I said. "I sure am out of the literary loop. I didn't know Steinbeck's son was a writer. What did he talk about?"

"He talked about his new book, *Down to a Soundless Sea*, and then he talked some about writing and about his dad."

"Oh? That must have been interesting." I blew across the surface of the hot tea.

"Sure was," Bonnie said. "Then he told a great story. It was about a time he was little and his dad got really pissed at him for something he did.

"The day of the incident, Thom got home from school and found a sealed envelope with a letter in it his dad had written to him. He knew before he started to read it that the letter would contain a whole litany of reasons why his wrongdoings were so terrible and another on how he should mend his ways.

"Thom told us he'd had to put up with reading three or more

pages about his bad behavior. Then he got to the end of the letter and read the postscript.

"It said, 'PS I'm sorry that I didn't have time to make this any shorter.'"

I grinned.

"The story was amazing," Bonnie said. "It captured the essence of good writing...*be succinct*. But God that's hard to do, Erica. It takes so much patience."

I sighed. "No kidding."

"Well, I guess that's what writing's all about—getting to the point," Bonnie said.

"It sure is." I put down my mug of tea and picked up my notebook.

"Wait," Bonnie said. "What question do you have about your book?"

"You just answered it."

Saying no more, we began to write.

After our meeting I went home and turned to my manuscript. I opened the section that was titled "The Law of Least Action."

I took the time to make it shorter.

INQUIRIES:

- **What is a waste of your energy?**
- **What is important?**
- **If you are a writer, look at a piece of your writing. Where can you trim the fat?**
- **What energy will be freed up when you say "NO" to a meaningless task today?**

SACRED ATTITUDE FIVE: SHOW UP

You must do the thing you think you cannot do.

—Eleanor Roosevelt

To come to life more fully,
So as to serve life more
wisely and more nobly.
Sagely stillness within.
Sovereign service without.

—John G. Sullivan

There is a vitality, a life force, an energy, a quickening, that is translated through you into action. And because there is only one of you in all time, this expression is unique and if you block it, it will never exist through any other medium and be lost. The world will not have it. It is not your business to determine how good it is, nor how valuable, nor how it compares to other expressions. It is your business to keep the channel

open. You do not even have to believe in yourself
or your work. You have to keep open and aware
directly to the urges that activate you.
Keep the channel open.
—Martha Graham

When we reach the point where it is more painful to suppress our passion than it is to take a risk and start expressing ourselves as if our lives depend on it, we claim our own authority and become the air-traffic controller of our own lives—we begin to *Show Up*.

By contrast, when we have a glimmer of an idea of what makes our own heart sing, and adopt the "I'm Not Enough Yet" attitude, we become stuck in a holding pattern on the runway of life. With our gifts hidden, the world is robbed of our light and becomes a much darker place.

We don't have the luxury of time to contribute to the darkness.

In her book, *The Four-Fold Way*, cultural anthropologist, author, and educator Angeles Arrien, Ph.D., writes, "Every human being carries the power of presence....Many indigenous societies recognize this capacity, often referred to as 'showing up' or 'choosing to be present and visible.' The power of presence means we are able to bring all four intelligences forward: mental, emotional, spiritual, and physical....When we choose to 'show up' energetically, with all four intelligences, we express the power of presence."

Magic Happens

When we *Show Up* in the world—just as we are—and give voice to what matters most to us, magic happens. I have seen that magic for myself, and I have seen it when my clients and friends take steps that make their own hearts sing.

Like the magic that happened when my client, Lisa, decided to take her beautiful voice out of the shower and into her community choral group. She got a lead part in a holiday production.

Or the magic that happened when my friend, Brian Lawless, spontaneously began writing Haiku poetry—he soon found himself with volumes of luscious material that he and his wife used to create exquisite, hand-crafted gift books.

Le coeur

Showing up takes courage—courage that's born of the *heart*. The French know this relationship well. The French term for "heart" is *le coeur—le coeur* also means "courage." It is a courageous act to stand by your heart.

My client, Jason, stood by his heart and transformed his life—he turned his weekend interest and passion for horses into a non-profit organization—one that takes at-risk kids on horseback treks.

My friend, Peller Marion, put her thriving executive-coaching practice on hold and committed to her love of writing. She dusted off her journals, wrote her heart out and approached agents. She is now the proud author of three published books.

My colleague, David, closed his medical practice in the city and traded it for a small-town three-day-a-week practice near the coast. He made more time to spend with his family and more time to comb the beach he loves; twice a week, he collects bits of polished glass at the shore and turns them into unique art sculptures.

My cousin, Lynn, stands by her heart and Shows Up every day to care for her young son. Doing so means the world to her. It also takes courage. Lynn had polio as a child and now has limited use of her arms.

Our Gift

Every day, life offers many moments for us to be more of ourselves—to bless the world with who we are and to be blessed by others—to *Show Up*. The questions life asks each of us in these moments include "Are you willing to stand by your own heart?" "Are you willing to touch life with your essential nature?" "Are you willing to give the world the gift of your *self*?"

This section captures moments when life offered a chance to those involved to *Show Up* more fully. I invite you to take the essays to heart and *Show Up* more fully in your own life.

WATCH FOR THE BLOOMING

Watch for the Blooming

It is spring
and blossoms of expectancy surround me
Quiet and full
I watch for the blooming.
Do you see it?

Over there
where the rose is opening to the sun
Over there
where the baby birds are hatching
in their robin's-egg-blue nests.

It is spring
and blossoms of possibility awaken in me
Quiet and full
I feel the blooming.
Do you see it?

There's no holding back this growth
no urgency to push this newness forward—
no need to make it summer
before its time.

It is spring.
And all around me there is blooming.

—ERK

In March, a few years ago, my colleague and friend, Peggy, came to my house for a lunch-time business meeting. Both of us had grown bored in our coaching practices during the winter months and we hoped a get-together would inspire us.

Peggy and I made tuna sandwiches and took them outside to the patio. We talked about our businesses while we ate. But it wasn't long before we got distracted.

A fat robin flew by, carrying bits of string to her nest.

Two noisy local squirrels scampered across the lawn.

The first blooms of pink jasmine sent their subtle spring fragrance to the patio table for our dessert.

"I love spring," Peggy said.

"Me, too."

We watched the robin make another trip to build her nest.

"The Chinese have the greatest way of thinking about spring," I said.

"How's that?"

"Well, they see spring for what it is. Not for what it's about to become."

"Tell me what *that* means," Peggy said.

"Are you sure? I can get long-winded about Chinese philosophy."

"Go for it," Peggy said. "I've got all afternoon. Plus, it gives me a chance to sit out here longer and enjoy the daffodils."

I finished a bite of sandwich.

"Okay," I said. "First of all, the Chinese don't see spring as a season that is only *external*."

"They don't?" Peggy said, "What do they include in their definition of spring?"

"In the world of Traditional Chinese Medicine (TCM), spring is a word used to describe an energetic reality that's *within* us as well as *all around* us. In the TCM system, the Chinese say that the seasons can be felt, seen, heard, smelled, tasted and are also actually evident in the body."

"They are?"

"Yup. Spring not only shows up as those plum blossoms over there, but it shows up inside of us. Spring is associated with a green tone to the skin, the emotion of snappy anger and the mental functions of planning and decision-making," I said, and brushed my remaining breadcrumbs on the patio for the birds.

"So, the Chinese don't just see signs of spring in the air, or trees, like we do," Peggy said.

"That's right. New business ventures, rising energy and growing excitement are all signs of spring in the TCM world view. But there's an even greater difference in the way the two cultures view spring."

"What's that?"

"In our culture, we don't honor or enjoy the spring season for what it is. We see new cherry-tree buds and say, 'Oh, look! School will be out soon.' We haven't even breathed in the blossoms' beauty and we're already anticipating summer."

"Oh I get it," Peggy said. She caught a fluffy wisp from a cottonwood tree as it floated by. "Spring isn't 'almost summer.' It's spring. It has its own life."

"Yes. That's how the Chinese see it. But they also say that every season is present within the season of spring—from the winter frost that's thawing, to the rising heat that is pregnant with summer," I said.

"What a paradox."

"Sure is."

"Well, I'm glad it's spring," Peggy said. "Full and magnificent spring."

"Me, too," I said. "I'm glad for the blooming lavender as *well* as for the new level of energy that's been blooming in my body lately."

"Since we're speaking of spring," Peggy said, "and how the dormant energy of winter is thawing out, why don't we begin a list of 'budding' new ideas for our businesses?"

"Cute," I said, rolling my eyes and grinning. "But not a bad idea. Let's do it."

We took pens from our notebooks and eased into spring.

***

Twenty years ago, a friend of mine wrote a short story called, "If You Are Pink, Be Pink." She wrote it to inspire the participants in her Life Purpose Workshop.

Judy was a master of metaphor and key words from her story still dance in my mind. "Pink is its own color," she wrote. "Pink shouldn't be described as 'not quite red.' Pink is pink. If you are pink, be pink!" Judy had strong feelings about honoring what is so.

I feel the same way about spring and the nature of spring within us. It is spring. There will be a time for fast action in the near future, but this is the time to watch the blooming—the time for noticing what is on the vine.

It is spring.

It is a precious time.

INQUIRIES:

- **What can you feel blooming in you?**
- **What is it to *be* with the blooming in your life—neither pushing things forward nor holding them back?**

THE ARENA

Early on in my midlife journey, I faced two challenges. I didn't know how to deepen my work with my clients. And I couldn't figure out what was missing from my writing.

I kept on writing anyway, one word at a time. I also kept up with my coaching practice, working with one client at a time. But like a lost puzzle piece, something was still missing. I did a lot of soul-searching as I struggled to discover just what that was.

A few years later, I received a gentle hint that helped me uncover what had been missing. Like finding a forgotten twenty-dollar bill in a winter coat pocket, I received an unexpected surprise—the gift of this dream:

> I enter an arena that is as huge as the Oakland Coliseum. I climb the stairs to what my friend Jennifer calls the nosebleed section. Halfway up, I find my reserved seat. I am by myself.
>
> Soon, other people arrive and make their way to their seats, too. Most of them are medical doctors and scientists. We are all filled with anticipation of a great evening program. The arena is filled with a soft hum of voices as people share their excitement about hearing the featured speaker.
>
> Then someone dims the overhead lights—the entire venue looks as if it is bathed in candlelight—and a hush settles over the crowd. In the center of the arena, a single spotlight casts a soft circle of

light on the wooden floor. I guess that the small, lighted area is where the speaker will be.

As I sit, I'm suddenly aware of something I need to say—something I need to say to the entire crowd. Without moving from my seat, I begin to speak.

"I know in my heart that what I have to say must be said, even though my words may not be eloquent, or nice, or what you may want to hear...but my message is mine to say and I'm here to say it anyway."

I don't recognize my voice. It's not loud, but it *is* full and deep and rich with passion—a passion that surprises me.

"I am proud to use alternative practitioners in my health care," I tell the crowd. "I believe that healing methods from the East are valid and helpful and not placebos." I speak right through the tears that are forming as I continue to talk about the things that are true for me.

"I believe that Western medical doctors don't have all the answers that they think they have. If they want their practices to survive this century, they'll need to embrace other ways of looking." As I say this, many of the doctors in the audience gasp. But I continue.

"I also believe that *attitude* plays a critical role in everything—in healing, in business results and in our daily lives. We need to be mindful of our attitudes."

As I speak, I note that the entire crowd is looking my way. My words and beliefs are controversial to many of the doctors and research scientists who have come to the arena. Some are aghast at what I say—shaking their heads in disagreement and rolling their eyes—they think I'm out of line. Others aren't yet sure what to make of this speech but are annoyed I've interrupted the evening program. I continue anyway.

"I believe that we are not only in danger of losing valuable plants from the rainforests but we are in danger of losing out on the valuable *human* gifts that are here on the planet as well," I say. "There is a global need for every one of us to bring our unique gifts forward. We do not have time to waste. We each need to follow our passion right now!"

It is getting harder to say what needs saying, but I do so because I must.

"The most dangerous attitude of all is the one we hold when we think we know it all—when we stop learning—when we don't continue to be curious. We adopt that attitude whenever we assign labels—even diagnoses—when we see only labels and diagnoses and stop seeing *people*."

At this, I see many people glaring at me. Some

are doctors and healthcare providers I've admired, respected and tried to please in the past. What I have just said doesn't fit their reality nor match their beliefs. One by one, they stand and leave.

My heart aches as I see the arena empty out. But through my tears, despite the feelings, I complete my truth-centered speech. "So while we *must* follow our hearts and bring our gifts forward, we also need to stay curious about the gifts that others bring—the strengths they bring—in their bodies, minds and spirits." Now, all of the seats that I can see are vacant.

Then I look behind me. Two people—an elderly couple—have stayed. They're intrigued by what I have to say and amazed that I've had the courage to say it. I realize that they have blessed me with their attention and presence, and I have blessed them, and myself, by speaking what's been mine to speak.

I awoke from the dream, knowing exactly what was missing from my writing and my coaching work: my voice—my passion—my willingness to say the words that are hard to say. Truthful words that might buck the system or push a few noses out of joint. Words of complete candor that might cause my clients to squirm or not *like* me. Authentic words—those that match my true feelings—that could alienate my family. I also knew when I awoke that it didn't *matter* anymore if my controversial opinions or honest words would upset some people—that I would speak and write the words that came from my deep heart.

This dream marked a big turning point for me. I had been pretty good about saying the tough things, but there were more layers of honesty I needed to bring forward in my life.

I needed to write with more honesty. My readers and I deserved no less. I also needed to give my clients more honest feedback when I saw them choosing attitudes that I knew were keeping them from leading more meaningful lives.

Speaking my truth in the arena of my life has since become a daily practice. And no matter who leaves, I know that I will continue to stay and speak from my heart—when I do, I'm often surprised to see that people choose to stay in the arena with me.

INQUIRIES:

- **What are you saying in the arena of your life at this time?**
- **What else do you want to do or say in the world?**
- **What is it to be supported in the arena of your life?**
- **Whose opinions have you allowed to hold you back?**
- **Perhaps it's not your time to speak in a new arena—perhaps it *is* your time to get up and leave an old one. Which arena no longer suits you?**

TENDING THE GARDEN

Facing my computer screen, I took a deep breath and prepared to get to work on my manuscript. My fingers were poised above the keyboard. I wanted to write that day. I hoped to write that day. I sat there. Nothing.

I had been overwhelmed by the enormity of my writing project for weeks, and I just couldn't move forward. I'd face the screen each day but my deep breaths led neither to inspiration nor to action. That day was no different.

In frustration, I checked my e-mail—I'd use any excuse to avoid the anxiety of staring at a blank screen.

I clicked open my in-box. Great, I thought, just one dumb forwarded message. I was about to trash it, sight unseen, but desperation for a distraction pushed me to open it anyway.

Seldom do I get a forwarded e-mail message that I think is worth reading—let alone sharing—but the following words spoke volumes to me that day:

The Daffodil Principle

by Jaroldeen Asplund Edwards

> Twice, my daughter Carolyn had phoned to say, "Mother, you must come see the daffodils before they are over."
>
> I wanted to go, but it was a two-hour drive from Laguna to Lake Arrowhead. Going and coming would take most of a day—and I honestly did not have a free day until the following week.

"I'll come next Tuesday," I promised, a little reluctantly, on her third call.

Tuesday dawned cold and rainy. Still, I had promised, and so I determinedly drove the length of Route 91, continued on I-215, and finally turned onto Route 18 to drive up the mountain. The summit was swathed in clouds, and I had gone only a few miles when a wet, gray blanket of fog covered the highway. I slowed to a crawl, my heart pounding.

The road became narrow and winding toward the top of the mountain. I executed each hazardous turn at a snail's pace. I was praying to reach the turnoff at Blue Jay that would signify I had arrived at my daughter's street.

When I finally walked into Carolyn's house and hugged and greeted my grandchildren, I said, "Forget the daffodils, Carolyn! The road is invisible in clouds and fog, and there is nothing in the world except you and these darling children that I want to see enough to drive another inch!"

My daughter smiled calmly. "We drive in this all the time, Mother."

"Well, you won't get *me* back on the road until it clears—and then I'm heading for home!" I assured her.

"I was hoping you'd take me over to the garage to pick up my car. The mechanic just called, and they've finished repairing the engine," Carolyn answered.

"How far will we have to drive?" I asked cautiously.

"Just a few blocks," she said cheerfully. So we bundled up the children and went out to my car. "I'll drive," Carolyn offered. "I'm used to this weather."

We got into the car, and my daughter began driving. In a few minutes I was aware that we were back on the Rim-of-the-World road, heading over the top of the mountain.

"Where are we going?" I exclaimed, distressed to be back on the mountain road in the fog. "This isn't the way to the garage!"

"We're going to the garage the long way," Carolyn smiled, "by way of the daffodils."

"Carolyn," I said sternly, trying to sound as if I were still the mother and in control of the situation, "please turn around. There is nothing in the world worth driving on this road in this weather."

"It's all right, Mother," she replied with a knowing grin. "I know what I'm doing. I promise. You will never forgive yourself if you miss this experience."

And so my sweet, darling daughter, who had never given me a minute of difficulty in her whole life, was suddenly in charge—and she was kidnapping me! I couldn't believe it. Like it or not, I was on the way to see some ridiculous daffodils—driving through the thick, gray silence of the mist-wrapped mountaintop at what I thought was risk to life and limb. I muttered all the way.

After about twenty minutes we turned onto a small gravel road that branched down into an oak-filled hollow on the side of the mountain. The fog had lifted a bit, but the sky was lowering, gray and heavy with clouds. We parked in a small parking lot adjacent to a little stone church. From our vantage point we could see, beyond us in the mist, the crests of the San Bernardino range like the dark, humped backs of a herd of elephants. Far below us the fog-shrouded valleys, hills, and flatlands stretched away to the desert.

On the far side of the church I saw a path covered in pine needles. Before us there were towering evergreens, riotous manzanita bushes, and an inconspicuous, hand-lettered sign: "Daffodil Garden."

We each took a child's hand, and I followed Carolyn down the path as it wound through the silent, giant trees. The mountain sloped away in irregular dips, folds, and valleys, like a deeply creased skirt. Live oaks, mountain laurel, shrubs, and bushes clustered in the folds, and in the gray, drizzling air, the green foliage looked dark and monochromatic. I shivered. Then we turned a sharp corner along the path, and I gasped.

Before me lay the most glorious sight! Unexpected and completely splendid. It looked as if someone had taken the great gold vat of the sun and poured it over the mountain peak and slopes, where it had run over every rise and into every crevice. Even in the mist-filled air, the mountainside was radiant with light, clothed in massive drifts and waves of daffodils.

The flowers grew in majestic swirls, great ribbons and swaths of deep orange, soft white, lemon yellow, salmon pink, rich saffron, and butter yellow. Each different-colored variety (I learned later that there were more than thirty-five varieties of daffodils in the vast display) was planted as a group so that it swelled and flowed like its own river with its own unique hue.

In the center of this dazzling display, a cascade of purple grape hyacinths poured down the slope like a waterfall of blossoms framed in its own rock-lined basin.

A charming path wound through the garden. There were several resting places, paved with stone and furnished with Victorian wooden benches and great tubs of coral and carmine tulips.

As if this were not magnificence enough,

Mother Nature added her own grace notes. Above the daffodils, a bevy of western bluebirds flitted and darted, flashing their brilliance. These charming little birds, sapphire blue with breasts of magenta red, danced in the air, their colors sparkling like jewels. Above the blowing, glowing daffodils, the effect was breathtaking.

It did not matter that the sun was not shining. The radiance of the daffodils was like the glow of the brightest sunlit day. Words, wonderful as they are, simply cannot describe the incredible beauty of that flower-bedecked mountaintop.

Five acres of flowers! (This too I discovered later.) "But who has done this?" I asked Carolyn. I was overflowing with gratitude that she had brought me here—even against my will. This was a once-in-a-lifetime experience. "Who?" I asked again, almost speechless with wonder, "and how, and why, and when?"

"It's just one woman," Carolyn answered. "That's her home." My daughter pointed to a well-kept A-framed house that looked small and modest in the midst of all that glory.

We walked up to the house, my mind buzzing with questions. On the patio we saw a poster with the headline, "Answers to the Questions I Know You Are Asking." The first answer was a simple one: "50,000 bulbs," it read. The second answer was,

"One at a time. One woman. Two hands, two feet, and very little brain." The third answer was, "Began in 1958."

There it was. The Daffodil Principle. For me that moment was a life-changing experience. I thought of this woman who, decades before, had begun—one bulb at a time—to bring her vision of beauty and joy to an obscure mountaintop.

One bulb at a time. There was no other way to do it. One bulb at a time. No shortcuts—simply loving the slow process of planting. Loving the work as it unfolded. Loving an achievement that grew slowly and bloomed for only three weeks of each year.

Still, by planting one small bulb at a time, year after year, this quiet woman had forever changed the world in which she lived.

I mused aloud. "What could I have accomplished had I approached some inspired project as this woman did?"

My wise daughter glanced at me with a smile. "Don't be discouraged. Start today."

She was right. We can choose a goal and begin to move toward it. By multiplying tiny pieces of time with increments of daily effort, we can accomplish magnificent things. We, too, can change our world.

***

When I finished reading the e-mail message, I opened my browser and surfed the net. Within one minute, I discovered that the "Daffodil Garden" is an actual garden in California and that the story in the e-mail had been copied—word-for-word—from Jaroldeen Edward's book, *The Daffodil Principle* (Shadow Mountain, 2004). Since the book was available on-line, I took a minute more and ordered a copy.

Then I sent a quick e-mail to Jaroldeen, asked for her permission to include the piece in this book, and went back to my writing with a renewed spirit.

One at a time, I planted the words on the page that needed planting that day.

I haven't missed many days since.

INQUIRIES:

- **How do you keep your dreams alive?**
- **What could you start right now that you've been putting off?**
- **Which activities, habits or beliefs do you need to weed out of your life?**
- **Where in your life do you resist beauty, joy or pleasure?**
- **What would you like to plant in the garden of your life?**

THE CAN OF PEARS

Most days last January, my mid-winter deadline for another draft of this book nudged me down the hall toward my computer at the crack of dawn. On one such trek, I passed my stagnant art table and felt my artistic muse give a noticeable tug on my sleeve. I can't make time for art right now, I thought. I'm deep into my writing project. I just can't.

But the muse kept a tight grip on me that morning and made sure I wandered over to the old art table several times. By noon I was longing to open my dusty boxes of watercolor supplies. By the end of the day I vowed to make time to paint again. The muse smiled.

The next day was Saturday. I didn't have plans so I made good on my vow. Switching on the white swing-arm lamp above my art table, I felt a stir of excitement. I gathered an assortment of my old paintbrushes, opened a watercolor exercise book I'd bought but never touched and sat down at my art table for the first time in a year.

Happy to be amid my tubes of Winsor & Newton watercolor paints again, I flipped through *Watercolor—A New Beginning*, by Ann K. Lindsay. The book looked like it held promise—and I figured I could use a new beginning.

I accepted the author's invitation to play and mixed up the juicy puddles of Alizarin Crimson, Ultramarine Blue and Lemon Yellow that she recommended. Swishing my brush in the water jar, I felt a grin spread across my face.

A few pages of watercolor paper later, I looked up at the clock above my table—three hours had disappeared. My grin turned to an annoyed scowl as I turned off the light and went to clean my brushes—I didn't want to leave my paints but my husband and I were meeting friends for dinner. At least there was comfort in knowing I'd paint again a few days later—I was hooked.

Twice a week for the next month, I came to my art table in the evening and splashed around in my watercolor paints. Each exercise in the book took me on a new adventure. I explored glazes, washes and colors, made twisting, twirling lines with my brushes and watched the paint dance as it met pools of water on the Arches paper.

In the evenings, I was in watercolor bliss—by day, the creative overflow moved onto my written pages and guided me gently toward my deadline.

One Friday night, anchored at my art desk, I read ahead to the upcoming watercolor exercise. "Explore a Pear in a Series," Ms. Lindsay beckoned.

The exercise asked me to experiment with creating an entire series of pear paintings—one pear on a page, one page at a time, as many paintings as I'd like. Oh boy, I thought. I love pears. I love drawing them. I love eating them. I love looking at them. I can't wait to do a whole series of pears and see what's different about each one. I'll start tomorrow.

On Saturday morning, I headed to the market. We didn't have one pear in the house and I wanted an assortment for my painting models.

I first selected two butterscotch-brown Bosc pears, figuring their curved stems and elongated necks would make graceful subjects. Then I added a few, bright, lemony-green Bartletts to my cart, remembering they'd ripen to a golden yellow in a few days—but wanting that classic pear shape no matter the color.

I already loved this painting exercise. As I added two Red Anjou pears to my cart, I admired their deep, rich, maroon color and large—almost egg-shaped—silhouettes.

What else? Ahh. Comice pears. I chose two bright-green beauties with small streaks of red blush on their short necks and added them to my basket.

The diverse pear collection was now large enough, so I headed to the checkout counter, paid for my treasures and drove home.

I placed one Bartlett on center stage of my art table, adjusted the lighting and began to mix my watercolor paints.

Then I peeled off a sheet from the block of 5x7-inch watercolor paper and turned to the illustrated pear exercise in the book. Checking the author's demonstration page, I read the reminder aloud, "Since I'm not making a painting there's no way I can ruin it. I'm simply exploring."

With that advice to encourage me, I dove in.

I dipped my brush into clean water and slopped it on the paper in a rough Bartlett shape. I dropped some Permanent Sap Green and Winsor Lemon into the water blotch and smiled at how close the color was to the actual fruit. As I set the first pear of my series aside, I gave myself a gentle reminder that the exercise was about playing and not realism.

I sat back and wondered just how playful I could let myself

get with the colors I used. Then my stomach growled. Giving a playful answer to my stomach's call, I reached over and grabbed a fat, tempting, blush-streaked Comice. I bit into the sweet, buttery flesh and licked the juice before it dripped down my chin. "I love this exercise!" I said, loud enough to reach across the country to Ann Lindsay's art studio.

I set my Comice core aside and moved the long-necked Bosc into the spotlight. Playful, I reminded myself, as I squirted a drop of Winsor Violet and Gold Ochre onto my palette. A few violet brushstrokes later and I could hear the purple pear giggle at me from the paper.

I continued to let my creative muse have complete reign and got lost in the watercolor process for three more delicious hours.

By the end of the day I had eight unique pear paintings—each one a reminder of the joy it had been to paint.

By the end of the following week I completed seven more juicy paintings to add to my collection—then I stepped back to look at the entire series of fifteen pears.

Each painting was beautiful, unique and stood in splendor amidst the variety that surrounded it—purple renditions; sap green, red, and turquoise versions; rounded, tall, lop-sided, and angular shapes. As I stood in pure delight I was filled with an urge to write about my pear-painting process.

I walked right over to my computer, switched it on and sat to write.

With my fingers resting on the keyboard, a loud, harsh voice began to scream in my head. It ranted, "You can't paint a series of pears and then write about the process."

I gulped and took my hands off the keyboard.

The I-Can't voice continued, "Sue Bender wrote about painting a series of pears in her book, *Everyday Sacred*."

I had an instant memory of a wonderful book I'd read a few years ago and gulped again.

"You can't write about pears. You're going to get arrested for plagiarism!"

This time I took a deep breath.

Glancing over at my fifteen pears, I reconnected to the joy I'd had in painting them.

Then I took another deep breath and reconnected to my passion for storytelling.

I placed my fingers back on the keyboard and wrote what was mine to write—the joy of painting fat, juicy pears and how their lusciousness had spilled over into my being during the last six weeks.

The I-Can't Monster disappeared once more. It couldn't interfere once I had given myself over the safety of my creative muse.

INQUIRIES:

- **What is yours to do that you must do no matter what?**
- **What stops you from expressing yourself?**
- **What will you have to say "yes" to, and what will you have to say "no" to, in order to express yourself more fully?**
- **What would it be like to *Show Up* and do something that gives you joy, even when your I-Can't-Monster tempts you to doubt yourself?**

A LOOK IN THE MIRROR

Earlier this evening, I called my friend, Naomi. I told her about the events of my morning, about the old man on the sidewalk and what I'd learned (the last essay in section three).

I explained to her that the events wouldn't have happened if I didn't have physical challenges right now and I hadn't cut down on my activities. "A few years ago, I wouldn't have had time to go to the post office in the middle of the morning," I said.

Naomi reminded me of something precious. "Erica, it wasn't the physical challenge you're dealing with that got you to see the old man needed help. The story is about you and how I've always known you."

"What do you mean?" I said.

"It's so like you to notice someone in need and be generous with yourself. Despite any limitations at the time, you show up and offer what help you do have to give."

Naomi's words brought tears to my eyes. I hadn't seen the story of the old man as a story about me. I saw it as a story about the gifts the old man gave to me...and that's why I'd shared it with her. The quick glimpse of myself through Naomi's eyes touched me. I could feel my own tenderness for myself.

We finished talking and said goodbye.

While doing dishes, I thought about Naomi's words. She was right. I do have compassion for others. And my time with the old man reminded me to practice the art of *self*-compassion as well.

As I continued to reflect on Naomi's words, I realized I disagreed with her on one important point: my physical limitations did play an important role in helping me see that the old man needed help this morning—they played the same role in all of my life.

By causing me to do less, I thought, my physical limitations have given me an opportunity to dig deep within—to uncover my heart—and find that there is more of *me* available these days. Imagine! And there I was, yesterday, feeling sad about my current limitations, feeling that there was less of *me* because I had less leg strength than I used to have.

What an amazing paradox, I mused, rinsing one last pot. The *payoff* in slowing down and doing less is to show up with more—more heart, more access to my intuition, more of my true self. I silently vowed to remember my morning with the old man whenever I needed to remind myself of that payoff.

I dried my hands, turned out the kitchen light and made one more promise as I left the kitchen—I'll remind myself often that my compassionate heart has been here all along...delighted to show up whenever I do.

Thank you, Naomi, for helping me see this.

INQUIRIES:

- **What shows up when you hurry less and wait more?**
- **What does a current limitation give you?**
- **What do you have to let go of for more of you to *Show Up*?**

THE TITLES WE WEAR

The first two years we owned our new home, life was busy and hectic. Along with our dream house, we'd purchased two major challenges: new home construction that was not quite complete, and a large yard without a scrap of landscaping.

I made more decisions during those first two years than I'd ever made before. Should we put in hardwood floors or carpeting? What would be a better investment—a concrete patio in the backyard or a redwood deck? My mental resources were taxed each day.

The house projects also made physical demands on me. I carried tiles home from Home Depot, lifted fabric samples in and out of my car and rearranged furniture—all the while monitoring my already existing health challenge.

My physical and mental energy were so consumed with new home projects, supervising teams of contractors and handling details I never knew existed, that I had to put my coaching practice on hold.

At first, the time away from my business was a blessing. I didn't have to worry over the questions I had about my coaching practice—and I had many—I could take a break from wondering: Do I really want to train new coaches to work with me or should I stay solo? What marketing plan makes the most sense this year? Where am I heading?

Instead, I was having fun expressing myself in new ways—solving the problems and making the choices involved in owning a newly constructed home. Could I find a refrigerator that would fit into the odd-sized allotted space in the kitchen? What type of bush would tolerate the direct afternoon sun in our western-facing front yard?

The projects were satisfying but whenever I stopped long enough to think, I became antsy—antsy about my title-less role. Who was I without a career title?

As the months went by, and the second year of projects began, my inner tension about the lack of a job title grew stronger. I faced that tension everywhere I went.

In the checkout line at Orchard Supply Hardware, the woman behind me shifted the 20-pound bag of fertilizer she was carrying to her other hip and said, "I'm a landscape designer. With all you're buying, you must be in the business...what do you do?"

I was at a loss for words—so I smiled, paid the clerk for my new garden hose and palette of plants and left the store—the helpful clerk who wheeled my purchases had to jog after me to catch up.

When I went to the Automobile Association to modify our car insurance policy a buxom clerk with drooping, gray hair repositioned her tortoise-shell hairclip and pointed to the triplicate form I handed her, "What's your job title? You left this space blank."

The omission hadn't been an oversight. "Oh, I'm not working right now," I said, even though I'd spent three hours that day choosing fruitless pear trees from Navlet's nursery, two more hours selecting Smokey Dutch Blue stain for the new concrete patio, had similar days lined up the rest of the week and all but collapsed into bed every night. That's what I really do these days, I thought. How do I list that on a form?

When I did have down time at the end of a day, I wrote in my journal about my inner quandary. *What do I call myself*? I wrote. *Do I tell people I'm on sabbatical? Do I say I'm a Project Manager? Am I a Designer*?

In between projects, my worries continued. When I had time for phone calls to friends, I often found myself saying, "Who am I? I work non-stop, but I don't have a job. Is my worth tied to earning money?"

One of those rare evenings, I talked to my friend, Bonnie, I gave her an updated report of my latest home projects...and then I shared my angst about my lack of a job title.

"Here's an idea for you," Bonnie said, donning the hat she'd worn for years when she was a practicing therapist. "Just observe your anxiety for awhile."

"What?"

Bonnie chuckled. "Keep having fun expressing yourself through your life choices, but observe your anxiety about having no title. Don't assign a label or title to yourself. Just notice the anxiety."

"Okay," I said, "I'll give it a shot. But this won't be an easy project."

"You've got plenty of practice with projects, kid. Have faith."

I trusted her and took on the challenge.

As the weeks went by, I practiced *noticing* the anxiety I had about not having a job title—and I continued to express myself through my new-home decisions and creative choices.

I designed our new front yard walkway, and chose a beautiful shade of sage-green paint for our walls. I also found a rhythm of resting and swimming that suited me—a rhythm that kept my body strong and stress-free.

As I focused on the joy of self-expression, my anxiety about not having a job title faded into the background. But I didn't realize it had. Not until one hot July afternoon.

My car was filthy from several trips to the nursery that week. Unpaved roads and parking lots left their dirty grime from one end of my car to the other. It was time for a trip to the car wash.

I gave my car keys to the car wash attendant at Autopia and paid for the Super Wash. Then I found a shaded spot out front where I could sit while I waited for my car.

The 94-degree heat, on top of my exhaustion, lulled me into a partial snooze. I was enjoying my mini-nap when the roar of a truck engine brought me back to consciousness.

A large, black, four-door super truck, with tires as tall as I am, came sliding out of the car wash tunnel.

I watched as a young car wash worker toweled off the truck, hoisted his falling-down jeans and went to look for the truck's owner. A minute later, from somewhere on the side of the truck that wasn't in my view, the truck owner strolled over to his truck.

Even with my truck-obscured view, I could see the strength of the truck owner's upper body. He had biceps as large as his truck tires, a gray ponytail hanging down his back and a tattoo of a bulldog on his left forearm. When he turned sideways to reclaim his keys, I also saw the front of his t-shirt:

TESTOSTERONE

Of course. The t-shirt said it all.

Five seconds later, Mr. Testosterone bent over and I lost my view of him.

When he stood up, he held two curly-haired, pink-ribboned little girls, one in each arm, and placed them onto the front seat of the truck. He leaned to fasten their seat belts and kissed each one on the top of the head.

Whoa. As the truck pulled away, I stared in disbelief. His t-shirt didn't tell me a thing.

That evening I called Bonnie.

I told her about my experience watching the truck owner at the car wash.

"Bonnie," I said, "I learned more about that guy by the tender way he treated those little girls than I ever did from his t-shirt."

Bonnie was quiet for a long moment.

"Erica," she said. "I know more about *you* by the excitement you have over your new sage-green wall and the pear trees you planted, than I would by any job title you will ever have."

"Me, too," I said, as contentment washed over me.

After the call, I wrote in my journal:

Dear Mr. Truck Owner,

I can see more of who you are by the actions you take, the choices you make and the people and things you love than I can by the title you wear.

Then I put down my notebook and smiled at my new sage-green wall.

INQUIRIES:

- **What do you want people to know about you?**
- **What actions can you take to reflect these values?**
- **What would your t-shirt say if it was a one-word description of your values?**
- **Where in your life can you make more room for the joy of self-expression?**

SACRED ATTITUDE SIX:
TRUST THE PROCESS

There is a Mystery, some call God, manifesting as a set of laws and a great process. And that process is perfect. That process also manifests itself in, as, and through me. And that process is perfect. As I come to know this more and more, in the journey of my life, I know that wherever I step, the path appears beneath my feet.

—Dan Millman

Be brave enough to live life creatively. The creative is the place where no one has ever been. You have to leave the city of your comfort and go into the wilderness of your intuition. You can't get there by bus, only by hard work and risk and by not quite knowing what you're doing. What you'll discover will be wonderful. What you'll discover will be yourself.

—Alan Alda

All I have seen teaches me to trust the creator for all I have not seen.

—Ralph Waldo Emerson

My husband is an avid whitewater river-rafting enthusiast. He often refers to the river as a metaphor for life. For example: I hadn't heard back from the panel of judges who had my writing-contest submission long past their two-month estimate—while I stomped around, griping about being unable to make them respond any faster, Steve reminded me, "Erica, you can't push the river." I hated him.

In another instance, I faced an unexpected health hurdle that caused me to put my coaching practice on hold. That time, Steve said, "Erica, you've got to maneuver around the boulders and go with the flow." I really hated him.

I didn't like hearing Steve's advice for either situation. But I knew in my heart he was right. In both cases, I was struggling against the current of life. In both cases, I forgot I could apply my own Sacred Attitude process—in the heat of those moments I didn't even consider that I could Stop...Look...Notice...and Choose to *Trust the Process*. Not at first.

<u>Timetables</u>

But in both situations, I finally did take Steve's river-advice to heart—I used it to remind myself to stop, take a few breaths, notice my resistant "attitude" and choose to *Trust the Process*—to let go of my timetable.

In the first instance, I chose to write a new article and submit it for publication rather than fret about the contest results or wear holes in the carpet with my pacing. This turned out to be a great choice: Although I got turned down by the contest judges, I found out the same week that my article had been accepted for publication.

When I chose to *Trust the Process* in the second instance, and surrender to the temporary health challenge, I traded my resistance for the chance to relax and enjoy the time off. I caught up on some reading and resting, spent "quality time" with the lavender in my garden and returned to my coaching practice refreshed, healthy and ready to go. A handful of unexpected clients showed up within very short order.

We waste precious energy whenever we paddle upstream. Learning to *Trust the Process* means learning to stop insisting on our own timetables—to trust that we are "right on schedule," in author Angeles Arrien's wise words.

Row, Row, Row Our Boats

The trick is to show up on the river of life, fasten our life jackets, grab our paddles and row our boats "gently down the stream."

Easy...when we have traveled the river before. Easy...when we are certain of the course we're taking. Easy...when we have extra vacation days to spend getting lost on the river.

But when the river is new to us, there is no map, or we are up against a deadline, remembering to *Trust the Process* becomes more of a challenge.

Arenas

There are many arenas where we can practice the sixth

Sacred Attitude—many opportunities for us to *Trust the Process*. From the artist's drafting table to the executive's boardroom. From the realm of corporate strategy to the world of new motherhood. From the classroom to the writing studio. Where are we tempted to try to force things along? How often do we get frustrated when things don't go "according to plan"? Are we addicted to over-planning?

No matter what river we travel, we don't always have to have a plan. The creative process, the process of life, has supported us all throughout the ages. It always will. We can let go and *Trust the Process*.

But make no mistake about it, deciding to *Trust the Process* will be a challenge for us...because we must also trust ourselves to discern when to let go and when to plan.

The essays in this section invite you to explore the realm of trusting the unknown—trusting the Mystery of Life—they invite you to *Trust the Process*.

Enjoy the river.

STAY ON THE BUS

I've kept dream journals since I was a kid. I've found over time that all of my dreams contain some kernel of wisdom worth considering. So, once in a while, I'll look through my old journals to see if there's a dream I've forgotten about that holds meaning for me today. But I don't need to review any journal notes to remember the following dream. I dreamed it in early October of 1989, but it seems like it was just last night:

> I'm a passenger in a large yellow school bus. I'm traveling somewhere, although the destination isn't clear to me.
>
> I sit on the green vinyl seat and stare out the window. I see city street signs, cars and buses going by, and people walking in and out of stores, but I'm not paying attention to other details. I do notice, though, that the streets are busy but quiet. So are the people. So am I.
>
> Then, BOOM! The sudden noise is deafening. The bus begins to rattle and bounce on its tires. I realize there's a massive earthquake.
>
> Now, from my window, I've suddenly got an aerial view of the whole earth. I can see the entire globe beneath the bus. I can see and feel the whole world shaking!
>
> After a few timeless moments, the earthquake stops. Everything is quiet again. But the yellow

school bus is in a precarious position.

Somehow the bus is bigger than the earth and is balancing on the top of the globe. It feels eerie to know we're teetering on the edge of the world. I panic.

I stand up on shaky legs. Should I go out the bus door? What should I do?

As I'm wondering, I hear the answer to my questions from someone with the most calm, soothing and loving voice I've ever heard. The bus driver, a very old and pleasant-looking gray-haired black man, speaks at the top of his voice, **"STAY ON THE BUS!"**

His tone is warm, authoritative and comforting. I'm glad someone knows what to do. His words put me at ease.

And so I sit, right there, and stay on the bus.

When I woke from that dream, I jotted notes in my journal and thought about the dream's message over the next few days. "Stay on the Bus" didn't appear to me like profound or earth-shaking advice but it did give me something to consider whenever any impulsive ideas crossed my mind, like ordering an extra-large bucket of popcorn at the movies. Other than that, it seemed like any other vivid dream I'd ever had. That is until two weeks later.

On October 17th, of 1989, I conducted a daylong workshop in

San Francisco. By 4:30 pm, I was glad to be finished and headed right to my car—comforted by the thought of taking a hot bath when I got home.

At 5:04, as my car inched its way through the traffic along a Bay Bridge on-ramp, I flipped on the radio to hear the news and the traffic report.

At 5:05, my car started bouncing and the radio broadcast stopped. I looked to my right and saw the cab beside me bouncing, too. In a flash I knew we were experiencing an earthquake.

I've lived in the Bay Area most of my life and am used to earthquakes. So I waited until the bouncing stopped and continued driving onto the bridge. The traffic was moving, but it was slow going.

Are people driving slowly because they fear an aftershock? I wondered. No, I'll bet there's an accident, I concluded. I tried the radio again in hope of hearing a traffic report. I still didn't get a signal. This was odd.

For reference, eastbound drivers, like me that day, head toward Oakland on the lower deck of the Bay Bridge, while westbound drivers, heading to San Francisco, use the upper deck. I crawled along with the traffic on the lower deck for about a mile.

And then traffic stopped moving altogether.

I sat in my car for fifteen frustrating minutes, as good as parked, a short distance from the mouth of the Yerba Buena Island tunnel. The bus that was parked in front of me, already halfway into the pitch-black tunnel, blocked my view ahead. From what I *could* see, I wasn't going to be moving any time soon.

After a few more minutes, the doors of the bus opened and passengers began to pour out and race-walk back toward San Francisco. I didn't understand why.

Then a young guy on a Harley motorcycle, who had ridden ahead to scope out the problem, came back toward the traffic jam shouting something as he navigated his way. I rolled down my window to hear him as he got closer.

"The bridge is out!" he screamed.

"What do you mean?" I hollered back.

He pulled his red and black motorcycle next to my window. "It's out. It's broken. It cracked. A section has fallen down from the top deck!"

My heart beat somewhere in my throat. The radio broadcast had still not resumed, and all I had to assess my situation were the words of a panic-stricken, perhaps delirious, motorcyclist. No, not just those words. I realized I had other information to use: passengers fleeing a bus to walk back to the city and an exit sign to the left of me that I'd never noticed in all my years crossing the Bay Bridge.

I don't make a habit of driving in the extreme left-hand lane of the bridge. Too close to the railing for me. I prefer to stay in the center.

Now who knows why, but on that day I was driving in the left lane, the lane that holds the single exit for Yerba Buena Island and its adjacent sister, Treasure Island. I was 25 feet from the only way off the bridge at that point, although I didn't know it at the time. All I did know was that my palms were sweaty and I was scared.

I took a deep breath. A calm within me took over and I knew

what to do. Stay on the bus, I remembered. The phrase now reminded me that I should avoid panic and drastic measures and go one step at a time.

I leaned out my window and asked the next passenger who exited the bus if he could tell me what was going on. What he told me I found hard to believe. The kid on the Harley was right. The upper deck of the bridge had cracked. A section had fallen onto the lower deck. The deck I was now on. A group of the man's fellow passengers had walked ahead to see it themselves and reported back.

Stay on the bus, I chanted within myself. Stay on the bus and keep breathing. I sized up this man in a flash, trusted the next inner guidance I got and took a risk. I offered him a ride back to the city in exchange for navigational directions. I didn't know if the exit could eventually lead me back to the city but somehow I thought he'd know.

He did. He also turned out to be a former structural engineer and knew a lot about bridges and what was happening. I found his knowledge quite comforting.

I wound up driving this man through the city, across two more bridges, and to his home and waiting family in the Berkeley area. Phone lines were out. I had no way to call my out-of-town husband and no idea if my own home was still standing; I accepted his family's offer to stay the night in their guest room.

The whole situation that day was miraculous to me. Between being in the only available exit lane, and not one foot closer to the cracked section of the bridge, to finding out that my passenger knew about bridges and structural integrity, I knew without a doubt that divine intervention was at work.

It also turned out, later that evening, that a relative of the man's family, a dispatcher for a police department, was able to get a phone line in to their home. This additional miracle let me make a call to my husband and my family to let them know I was safe.

I don't make a habit of picking up hitchhikers or people getting off buses. Nor do I spend the night in homes of people I've never met. But some things bring us all closer together. Some things let us know there is one earth and we really are all family. Some things come along and shake our world in unexpected ways.

In those times, the words of the bus driver may well be the wisest words we can use to help us trust ourselves and trust the process of life: STAY ON THE BUS!

INQUIRIES:

- **Where in your life would it help you to "Stay on the Bus" right now?**
- **During the tough times, we often don't see the gifts in the situation—the "left-hand exits" or the "helpful bus passengers" who are right in front of us. This week, look around you. What gifts are present in your life?**

JOURNEY INTO THE PIT

It is summer. The pace of life is quick, and laughter and play are all around me. From my open kitchen window, I watch our next-door neighbor's ten-year-old daughter, Emma, practice her softball fast-pitch with her dad. But my own speed is not so fast today.

I bite my lower lip to keep the welling tears in check and bend down to rub my calf muscles. As I touch my skin I whisper my mantra, "Blessed am I to live in the sacred temple of my body." Then I turn and take slow steps to the backyard.

Taking a seat in a webbed patio chair, I feel the afternoon August sun warm my skin.

I hear our backyard-neighbor Jan's grandchildren squeal with laughter as they splash around in Jan's swimming pool. The kids are immersed in joy.

But sadness pulls at my heart as I realize the backyard setting hasn't changed my reality. I rub my tingling palms together as I repeat my mantra, "Blessed am I to live in the sacred temple of my body." I see that while I'm a short 100 yards away from the sights and high-spirited sounds of summer, I'm sitting in a different season.

I am in an emotional and physical winter.

This is a difficult season for me, I think. Difficult to be here in this place where my legs aren't doing what I want them to do—where I can't tell what I'm touching unless I look, and then see it is my own thigh. Where it takes a long time to urinate, and where tingling and numbness have replaced the sensation of my jeans against my skin. It is difficult to know that my body is in hibernation right now, while the vibrancy of summer is all around me.

"Blessed am I to live in the sacred temple of my body," I say as I go inside to write in my journal.

I want writing to help me face the winter of my soul.

I find a pen and my notebook and sit to write.

We build the foundations of our lives with things and people we think we can count on—our friends, our families, our careers. It's tough when we can't count on our bodies. It's tough for me not to be able to count on mine. Can't count on it to be the same from one moment to the next, or from one day to the next.

I stop writing and take a sip of water, pulling a box of tissues closer to my notebook.

"Blessed am I to live in the sacred temple of my body," I say as I begin to sniffle.

Back to my writing. A single tear smears the ink.

This is tough work, this physical challenge. In fact, it sucks. But I don't want to write about this in my book. No one will want to read about the struggle.

My physical woes will depress people, and there is plenty of that in the world. Besides, I don't like reading other people's self-centered accounts of their health challenges. It seems indulgent.

And who cares that some unknown person faces some malady or another? Unless you are a celebrity—like Michael J. Fox or the late Christopher Reeve—why would anyone want to know that someone out here is struggling just to pee or tie her shoe in the morning? Who would care that I have to deal with wearing unflattering Mary Jane shoes and that there are no high heels in my closet or charming little pumps that Oprah says are her favorite? Why would anyone want to read about the deep dark emotions of my darkest days?

The writing is working. Tears are pouring down my face now. I have opened up the floodgates of despair. I take a deep breath and keep writing.

Well, to hell with it—maybe people like to read about happy stuff, and pretty things, but the physical symptoms I face are not happy or pretty. And even though the masters of Tai Chi and positive thinking say to focus on the good stuff of life, I think it's important to go into the pit of despair if that's what you face. Even if you don't know where the pit will lead.

I push my writing aside. I see that the pit of despair is what I face right now. And I know I must walk the talk of what I've just written. I've been dancing around the despair.

Going forward takes all the courage I can muster.

Sitting on the floor, I give in to my grief. The sobs shake my soul and tire my stomach muscles.

I've entered the pit.

I can smell the moldy terror that lurks on the walls of the place. I think I'll probably die here. But I stay anyway.

I begin to wail. I am filled with sadness, anger, disappointment, fury, and fear. I roll around in it for a while.

Still crying, I look out my open bedroom window. The flowers outside are so bright next to my darkness, and the children's laughter from Jan's yard is so melodic next to my sobs, that I feel even worse.

"Blessed am I to live in the sacred temple of my body," I shout.

I pound my open palms on the carpet.

"Bull! I don't feel blessed. This isn't fair. I want to be having fun, moving around, enjoying the summer."

Snot runs from my nose but I don't care. Crying is now beginning to feel good.

Before I realize it...something shifts. I feel filled by my sadness and anger.

Soon, the sobs are less. I'm not thinking much and my breathing is slow and rhythmic.

I get up from the floor, decide I will take a shower and, as I take one slow step at a time, give thanks I can walk to the bathroom.

Lifting each foot to wash is an accomplishment today.

After my shower, I stand nude in front of our full-length mirror and repeat my mantra, "Blessed am I to live in the sacred temple of my body." Three times.

With each statement, I brush my hands over my body. I have learned from Qigong (Chi Kung) master Roger Jahnke that in doing so I am massaging my own Chi (life-force energy). As if taking a shower without water, I slide my hands over my arms from my fingertips to my torso, and from my toes up to my face. Up the front of me and down the back. As I do, I continue to say, "Blessed am I to live in the sacred temple of my body."

But it takes me saying the mantra and doing the Chi Bath *five* times today before tears of sweetness come and I mean what I say—and mean it with my whole heart—that if there is anything I have in this world, it is a deep reverence for life and for the life of my body.

A sixth time I say, "Blessed am I to live in the sacred temple of my body."

I am at peace and still. I am looking at my body with love. This journey has been a gift to my body and soul.

Sometimes my journeys into the pit of despair last a few minutes...sometimes a few days. Today, it seemed endless, but it wasn't.

My journey is over for now. A sweet tenderness envelops me...the gift of staying with my process and traveling where I need to go.

The sweetness now holds me.

Blessed am I.

INQUIRIES:

- **What would it be like to view your body, the way it is right now, as a sacred temple?**
- **Where in your life do you resist going into the pit?**
- **What might become available to you if you journey there?**
- **When you take a "Chi Bath" each day and affirm that you are blessed to live in the sacred temple of your body—no matter what it looks like, nor how it functions—you affirm life. My clients tell me that doing so is a life-changing process for them. What happens for you when you do the same thing for a week?**

FINDING MY OWN WAY

Finding My Own Way

No meandering river
lazy and inviting on a summer's day,
this path has been hell at times

Overgrown with signs
that point in different directions
are many illusions.

The wild calls out
screeching voices echo in the forest
often the bushes have thorns
their sweet fragrance missing

I can only listen to
the sounds of my heart
I can only trust
that the path is below my feet
I can only believe
in the meaning of my journey.

—ERK

INQUIRIES:

- **What path is calling you?**
- **What thorns are you tolerating?**
- **What does your own heart tell you?**
- **What does it mean to trust?**

A SAFE ADVENTURE

The majority of my clients are grappling with midlife struggles. While reassessing what is important, making career shifts, and sending their youngest children off to college, they try to make sense of the second chapter of their lives.

This stage of life is a messy business. I know it well. I am also between selves. I still have no idea what I'm creating on this canvas of my life. As my clients do, I have many unclear and uncertain moments. But there's a favorite childhood memory that comforts me.

When I was eight, we took a family vacation to Disneyland. I'd been before and I looked forward to seeing the Magic Kingdom again.

When we arrived, I ran through the entry gates and hugged Mickey. Throughout the day, I found Disneyland to be as wonderful as ever. Well into the night, Disneyland kept its promise of magic. But things had changed since our last visit.

As we walked toward my favorite ride, a small but distinct sign grabbed my attention:

Welcome! Please excuse our mess—

This attraction is being completely refurbished.

A brightly colored drawing of Mickey, sporting a pair of carpenter's overalls and holding a hammer and nails, illustrated the message. The captivating sign helped me add a new word to my vocabulary. Refurbished.

My Dad gave a further explanation and then herded us into line. We endured a forty-five-minute wait with other kids and families who weren't put off by Mickey's warning.

When we got inside we overlooked the boards, the scaffolding in the background and the strips of yellow plastic tape that sectioned off the work zones. We were excited to get to the front of the line and to hear the familiar music.

I guess we trusted Walt Disney. Despite the refurbishing signs, we climbed right into those little wooden boats. Off we went, expecting nothing less than a grand time. And that is what we had.

When we got out, we talked about the magical characters, the music, the swift rapids that the boats navigated, and how we couldn't wait to come back. We trusted that any Disneyland ride being refurbished, no matter if it looked messy right now, would somehow turn out to be an even better ride when we came back...even if it looked different from what we'd known. After all, it *was* the Magic Kingdom.

So I wonder, why don't we sit back in our midlife boats and trust the "Magic Kingdom" of life?

Seen in this light, the midlife struggle seems less daunting. Seen in this light, I am more able to relax into this journey, and so are my clients. Seen in this light, we may even be able to enjoy the ride.

INQUIRIES:

- **What is it to view midlife as a safe adventure-vehicle in the "Magic Kingdom"?**
- **What would change if you were to trust that you are "right on schedule"?**
- **When something baffles you, and you can't figure it "the hell out," what helps you relax into the unknowing?**

SACRED ATTITUDE SEVEN

BE WITH THE QUESTIONS

Some people will never learn anything...
because they understand everything too soon.
—Alexander Pope

Sometimes questions are more
important than answers.
—Nancy Willard

Men cannot live without mystery.
He has a great need of it.
—Lame Deer

At one point in my life, when the western medical community initially couldn't make up its mind about how to diagnose my physical symptoms, I struggled with the period of unknowing. At the time, my acupuncturist, and life mentor, the late Hal Bailen, M.D., said, "Why do you need a label?"

His question left me speechless. What would I gain from a

label?

I took a deep breath and decided to *Be With The Questions* rather than force answers.

I have lived with Hal's question for sixteen years. It has taken me into some rich territory. The question has had me consider the limitations of labels and how I stop learning once I put people, or situations, into categories.

The practice of living with Hal's question—"Why do you need a label?"—also had me consider other questions. What is it not to know? What else opens up when I live with a question for a while?

Now, even when the medical debate continues about which label—MS, residual back challenges from an auto accident, or some other phrase—fully explains the symptoms I have, the world opens up for me when I live without a label—when I live with questions.

The Juice of Life

I think the place of unknowing is where the juice of life is. To practice living in this place is to practice staying curious and to embrace the Sacred Attitude, *Be With The Questions*.

Imagine. What if we practiced living with questions each day?

What if we lived in a world where we were rewarded for not knowing?

What if curiosity and unknowing were encouraged?

What if there was a quiz in school where students were asked to list all the questions they have about life?

What if you had to write an article or give a speech about what you don't know?

I think I would learn more about you if I asked you what you *don't* know and what questions you are living with, than if I asked you to tell me all you *do* know.

Yes, there are times when knowing an answer to a question is vital. If you dial 9-1-1, and the operator asks you for information to help assess your situation, including your location, it's not time to tell the operator that you'd rather just *Be With The Question* for a while.

A Call to Courage

While it takes tenacity to pursue answers in this world, it takes courage to *Be With The Questions*. Perhaps that call to courage leaves us uncomfortable and has us rush to grab on to answers. Perhaps it is time we learn to value another way of operating. Perhaps there is even more to be learned in the moments of unknowing.

The essays in this section invite you to embrace the seventh Sacred Attitude—to *Be With The Questions*—to stay curious and, through exploration, gain more comfort living with the questions of your own life.

Notice that the word "question" itself contains an invitation—an invitation to go on a "quest." Let the questions at the end of each essay in this section take you on a journey—And if you go with an open heart and an open mind, you may wind up in places you've never imagined.

WHAT'S IMPORTANT NOW?

In 1991, my friend Jeff headed for home after an international business trip, expecting to take a nap when he arrived. Instead, he found his home had burned to the ground in the Oakland Hills fire.

Last year, my colleague, Kent, a new father and CEO of a major corporation, went to his doctor for his annual physical exam. He expected a clean bill of health. A few days later his doctor called to tell him he had lymphoma.

A year ago, my forty-six-year-old cousin, Shari, asked her husband to pick her up from work. They were going home to have a quiet dinner together. On the way home, Shari died of a heart attack in the car.

Sometimes, while we are going along minding our own business, life intervenes and throws us a curveball. For some people, like those above, the curveball appears in the form of a major life setback. For other people, the curveball shows up as a windfall of good fortune—like a large lottery prize, a significant salary increase, or meeting the love of your life on a cruise ship.

My client, Nancy, was a weekend-artist for years. This year, on a whim, she decided to submit her ceramic sculptures to a local art show. She was expecting her pieces wouldn't get accepted. The next thing she knew, she had so many orders for her artwork she had to decide if she could keep her day job—a tough decision since she loves it as much as she loves making art.

Regardless of the form they take, curveballs are sudden and unexpected events that forever change us. They entail some sort of a loss—the loss of the familiar—as well as a new chapter. And at some point, we recognize that we have entered into uncharted territory with a suitcase full of questions.

Some of the questions left in a curveball's wake have no answers...and learning to live with unanswered questions is big work for us in this culture.

A big curveball came onto the planet on September 11, 2001. That afternoon, I called my friend, Joyce. We didn't have much to say to each other at first. We just listened to each other breathe.

After a while, I said, "My God! We've had more questions placed before us today than we ever asked for."

"Well, we certainly have more questions now than we have answers for," Joyce said.

"Yeah. I guess all we can do is count our blessings."

"You're one of mine," Joyce said.

"You, too," I said, wiping my drippy nose on my sleeve.

We talked a bit longer and said goodbye. Later we learned that we each went to the kitchen and made our families a large pot of soup.

That night, I had this dream:

> An old Chinese master, wearing black silk robes, sat in the front of a high school auditorium. The world had just been hit by a disastrous tidal wave that wiped out entire cities. Everyone left was shocked and sad. We'd come to the auditorium to get the wise man's counsel.
>
> "Tell me about the tidal wave," the wise master

said.

"We weren't expecting to lose our families. We're in shock," a young mother in the audience said, twisting her orange scarf.

"I'm pissed. My car got swamped," a lanky teenaged boy said.

"What else?" The elderly sage spoke to the audience. "How else do you feel?"

A man wearing a grey pinstripe suit and fighting back tears said, "I lost my twin brother and I hurt real bad. My stomach feels like a lead ball is sitting inside."

"Okay," the wise man said. "What else?"

A middle-aged woman stood up, her face twisted into an angry grimace. "I just don't understand why this happened to us. What will become of the world now?"

The old man stood and looked out into the audience. He made eye contact with each one of us in turn. Then he spoke. "There are no answers to the questions you have," he said. "You must ask yourselves a bigger question and just sit with it. You must ask yourselves, what is important now?"

Then the old man left the auditorium, disappearing into the night in his long black robes.

I woke up. The dream still floated in my mind. I turned to look at my sleeping husband beside me and felt as though we'd actually been to see the old man in the dream and had just gotten home. I kissed Steve on both cheeks and grabbed my journal from my nightstand. I wrote down notes from the dream and then I wrote:

How do we know what's important now? I think the discernment process is different for each one of us. My own way of telling what's important isn't easy to ignore—I get a definite physical feeling—a strong, reverberating gong of certainty...right in the center of my belly. When I experience this feeling, there is no question that the person or situation is important to me...it's the way I feel about Steve, my close friends and family, and my work in the world.

I stopped writing and thought about the conversation I'd had the day before with Joyce.

"My way of knowing what's important is to listen for a quiet whisper," Joyce had said. "When I hear a soft, 'yes,' that's when I know something's important. I'll be outside for a morning walk, and the trees seem to say, 'yes.' Or I'll be holding Michael and Jenna (her children) and the sweet scent of them says, 'yes' to me."

I went back to my writing. *Gong or whisper*, I wrote, *I guess life is telling us this is a good time to pay attention to what's important now.*

I put down my pen, kissed Steve again and got out of bed to go make breakfast. Simple eggs and toast for the two of us were all that was important.

Perhaps curveballs are nature's way of getting us to clean out the closets of our lives and uncover our values. The events of September 11th have had me clean out mine. I ask myself again, what is important now? The question seems to be a good one to ask every day.

***

Authors note:

I wrote this essay a month after the events of September 11, 2001 and the dream I'd had that night. I had no idea how relevant the dream's message would come to be. As we head to press with this book, this country is reeling from the impact of two more curveballs—Hurricanes Katrina and Rita. The words of the Chinese sage were an anchor for me the past two weeks, while I worried about property we own on the Gulf Coast—they helped me focus on the important things. Thankfully, we have been fortunate to incur negligible damage to our property. Thousands of other people were not this fortunate. The sage's question, *"What's important now?"* led me to ask myself another question: What can I *do* now? I put my answer, in the form of a donation, into an envelope and sent it to the American Red Cross for Hurricane Relief. Sometimes curveballs bring clarity.

INQUIRIES:

- **What's important at this point in your life?**
- **What people or activities add a delicious spice to your life?**
- **What is no longer important?**

CIRCLE OF WISDOM

My writing was stale, the words didn't sing and I found no redeeming qualities in anything I'd written for a week. I shut off my computer and tossed the pages I'd just printed into the trash. I stomped out of my writing studio with my inner critic on my shoulder telling me to give up writing and find a different creative outlet.

As a new week unfolded, I found a million excuses to avoid the blank page—then I had a million harsh adjectives to describe my behavior. Final score at the end of the week? Inner Critic: two million—Me: zero. I hated my writing. I hated my hair. I hated the world.

A few days later, still hating my life, I spoke with my coach, Craig Carr. While I lamented about my terrible writing, my lousy mood and my plans to find a new avocation, Craig listened.

Then, as we ended our telephone session, Craig offered me an inquiry to consider for the upcoming week. "See where this question takes you," he said. "What is it to have compassion for yourself?"

Craig's question percolated in the background of my mind all week. While doing the laundry, I considered the question. While driving to and from client meetings, I tossed the question around in my mind. And when I swam laps, I silently chanted with each lap: What is it to have compassion for myself?

The urge to come up with an answer was as tempting as chocolate, but I resisted. I knew that staying with the question was valuable. After my second swim that week, I packed up my swim gear and continued wondering, what it was to have compassion for myself. As I left the locker room and drove home, a twinkle of an idea began to dance across my mind.

My art materials were the twinkle that called to me and I wanted to answer them in a hurry. I walked in the front door, headed straight for my office and cleared a space on my art table. I knew just how to go deeper into the question I'd been pondering. I'd draw a Mandala to gain more insight and "see" where the inquiry would take me.

"Mandala" is the Sanskrit word for circle. But Mandalas are more than just circles. They are round drawings—often containing elaborate designs—that are compelling to draw and more compelling to observe. They are keepers of unexpected wisdom.

In her book, *Mandala*, author Judith Cornell explains, "Mandalas focus and reflect the spiritual content of the psyche for both maker and viewer." Years ago, in art therapy school, I'd also learned that the Mandala—often seen in Native American sand paintings—is considered to be a healing and transformative art form. The sacred circles are used in Hindu and Tibetan Buddhist rituals, as well as in modern psychotherapy.

The process of drawing and reflecting upon Mandalas can clarify many of life's turning points and questions. Through the years, my clients and I have seen that process play a definitive healing role in our lives. After a week of wondering what it is to have compassion for myself, I knew it was a good time to draw a Mandala.

I put a cassette of classical music into my tape player and took my old cigar box full of colored pencils down from the shelf. I put the box and a large sheet of white paper on my art table.

Sitting down, I closed my eyes and centered myself by taking a few deep breaths. Craig's question came to the foreground of my mind. What is it to have compassion for myself? I opened my eyes and began to draw.

First, I traced around an old Tupperware lid to sketch an eight-inch circle. Then I rummaged through the box of colored pencils and, without thinking much, chose colors that felt like they reflected compassion—soft blues, a gentle lavender and four soothing shades of green.

Starting at the perimeter of the circle, I drew rounded shapes, sweeping lines and curved arches of color. As Pachelbel's "Canon in D" played in the background, I got lost in the drawing. Craig's question disappeared.

By the time my colors and shapes reached the center of the circle—completing my Mandala—the tape ended. The only sound left in the room was the soft rhythm of my breathing. The frown that had been between my eyebrows for the last week had disappeared and my shoulders were relaxed for the first time in days. I pushed my chair back and stood to stretch. It was time to step back and observe my Mandala.

Staying interested and curious rather than harshly judgmental is no easy task for me when I look at my own artwork. As I stood before my Mandala that day, I knew the secret was to stick with simple observation.

First I noticed the colors of the Mandala—the soft greens and cool blues sat side by side in one area and blended together in another. Then I observed the shapes within the Mandala—sharp lines and edges at the perimeter and softer, rounded shapes toward the center. Gazing a bit longer at the Mandala, I realized I was smiling.

I hung the drawing above my writing desk, turned off the light and closed the door.

When I came into my office the next day, I glanced at the Mandala. The cerulean blues, marsh greens, and gentle, curving, leaf-like patterns greeted me. As I stared at the drawing I wondered—What is it to have compassion for myself? I let the spirit of the Mandala and the inquiry enfold me as I sat at my computer.

Words tumbled out of my heart, poured right down through my fingertips and made their way onto the screen. I let them flow without judgment, but I was amazed. Was I the same person who could not find one word to write last week? I didn't think so. The Mandala cast a sweet, soft beam in the background as the words kept flowing. Later, when I looked over my writing, I found things I liked—words that sang and sentences that worked.

When I spoke with Craig the following week he said, "Well, where did the inquiry take you?"

I glanced at my Mandala and smiled again. "Well, Craig, I'm enjoying myself and my writing. I've glanced at my Mandala when I've been tempted to judge my work, and stopped to breathe instead. It seems compassion has come from steeping myself in the question, not from forcing an answer."

"Nice work," Craig said.

After that, every time I looked at the drawing it reminded me to stay with the spirit of self-compassion. I knew the inspiring image would remain on my wall for a while longer.

When it was time, I would add the Mandala to the others I'd drawn over the last ten years. I keep the collection in a notebook and glance at it now and then. When I look back, I'm reminded of all that these sacred circles have taught me.

INQUIRIES:

- **What questions do you want to explore today?**
- **What is the color of your question?**
- **What is it to have compassion for yourself?**

PASSPORTS

One day last fall, my client, Wendy, a high-energy redhead in her early 50's, walked into my office for her twice-monthly coaching session. That day, she had an extra spring in her step.

Wendy hung her purse and sweater on the wooden coat rack, poured herself a mug of tea and flopped into the green wingback chair she'd claimed as her own over the last six months.

With a file folder in one hand and my mug of tea in the other, I closed the door with my shoulder and sat in the wingback chair facing her. "So, how are you?" I said.

A broad grin stretched across Wendy's pixie face. "Remember how overwhelmed I was when I came for our last session?"

"You bet. I remember asking you 'What questions are you living with?' and you told me about the bucketful you were carrying around."

Wendy laughed. "No kidding..."

I put my file folder down and listened.

"I was living with plenty of questions," Wendy said. "My youngest daughter had just left for college three days before, Jeff and I were signing closing papers that evening on our first investment property, and I was starting a new editing job the next day."

"You were living in unknown territory," I said. "But you're beaming today. What's happened?"

"Well, when I was here last time, I swore I had too many questions in my life and not enough answers," Wendy said, "but I left here with yet another question...remember?" She smiled and took a sip of tea.

I glanced at my notes. "Ahh. The inquiry you said you'd ponder was, 'What do all these questions hold for me?' "

"That's it all right," Wendy said, sitting upright. "At first, I didn't even have time to remember the question let alone consider it. But three days later, I got a chance to remember it big time. Listen to this!"

Wendy put her mug down, sat on the edge of the wingback and told me her story. Her explanation was so rich with detail, I asked her later if I could write it up in story-form:

While We Were Waiting

by Wendy T.

A week after I started my new job, my boss, Ted, announced a new project for our computer magazine at our company-wide staff meeting. "I'll explain the details to the creative team tomorrow," he said.

Ted's creative team consists of four people: Pat, the art director; Dirk and Robin, the two senior writers; and, as editor, me.

The next morning, all five of us, Ted included, headed to the boardroom.

As soon as we sat down, a loud metal banging sound began to fill the room.

"What's making all the racket?" I said.

"A construction crew's been working on the floor above us," Pat said. "They were here last week.

I guess they're back."

Ted stood up. "Okay, guys," he said, "we're out of here. Let's go down to the conference room on the ground floor."

In a heartbeat, we left the boardroom, took an elevator down to the ground floor lobby and marched into the conference room. Ted closed the door, I silently thanked God for the peace and quiet, and the five of us had a great meeting.

Afterwards, we headed back to the bank of elevators and waited for a ride to our offices. When the elevator arrived, all five of us got on board—and so did a bicycle messenger kid who scrambled in behind us just as the doors started to shut.

Robin pushed the sixth floor elevator button, still talking about the success of our meeting. The messenger leaned over and pressed button number four. When the doors closed, we observed customary silence and waited for lift off.

But, the elevator didn't move.

So Ted pushed the sixth floor button—I guess he thought that another time would help.

Nothing happened.

He pushed the button for the doors to open.

Nothing happened.

Then, the lights dimmed.

"Damn it," Ted said. "What's going on?" He pressed the red intercom button on the emergency panel. "All lines are busy now," a synthetic voice said. "Please try again later."

"Great," Ted said.

"*Now* what?" I said, beginning to worry.

Pat said, "I have a cousin who was stuck in an elevator once. He was fine. We just have to wait."

"You know," Dirk said, "I thought I saw one of the construction guys on his walkie-talkie as we went through the lobby."

"He was probably doing something with the power for the guys up on the sixth floor," Robin said.

Ted pressed the intercom button again.

The recorded voice answered. "All lines are busy now..."

"All the elevators must be out," Ted said. "I'll bet that's why the lines are busy."

I felt sweat trickle down my forehead. "How do we get air?"

"No problem," Pat said. She pointed to the vents at the top of the elevator. "My cousin told me elevators aren't air tight—air circulates through them all the time, just like it does in the rest of a building."

The messenger kid stomped his foot and said, "Man, if I'm late with this delivery, my boss will *shoot* me. How long is this gonna take?"

"We'll find out, buddy...just hang tight," Ted said,

sounding surprisingly calmer than he had a moment before—it must have been a fatherly thing. He pressed the intercom button again.

This time, a live person spoke. "Maintenance, Mike Townsend."

"Mike, it's Ted Sweeney, from *Nuevo Times*. We're stuck in an elevator on the ground floor. What's the story?"

"We're on it," Mike said. "Seems the construction boys were turning circuit breakers off and on again down here to find which one affected the upstairs crew. One of their off-again-on-again experiments must've done something to the elevator. We called the elevator repair guys and they're on their way."

I leaned toward the intercom and asked Mike, "What's that mean for us?"

"Just keep waiting. They'll be here," Mike said.

"How long will these lights stay on?" Robin said.

"The emergency lights are good for four hours," Mike said. "But we'll have you moving sooner than that."

"Thanks a lot, Mike," Ted said. "But try to make it lots sooner. Okay?" He released the intercom button and shook his head.

The messenger kid mumbled something and sat down on the floor. Dirk shrugged and joined him. So did Robin.

"Good thing it's blue-jeans Friday," she said.

I sighed, said, "What the hell," and sat down too.

Ted and Pat settled in for the wait by leaning against the railing on the back wall.

In the frustrated but resigned silence, not knowing when we'd move, I realized circumstance had just added another unknown to my already unsettled life.

Then I remembered the question from my last coaching session—*What do all the questions I'm facing hold for me?*

A humorous idea entered my mind. I figured being stuck in an elevator was a good time to explore the gifts of the unknown. I laughed and broke the silence.

"Hey," I said. "In addition to wondering when we're getting out of here, what other questions are you guys living with in your lives?"

"What do you mean?" Dirk said.

I looked up at him. "In other words, what *don't* you know right now?" I sat back against the side wall. "I'll bet finding out what people *don't* know is a good way of getting to know them better."

Ted chuckled. "A social icebreaker in a dead elevator? That's one for the record books."

"The only thing I don't know," the messenger kid said, "is why I ever took a break from law school to deliver mail. At least the elevators at Boalt never got stuck."

"And we don't know your name," Pat said, looking at the messenger.

"Hank," the kid said, smiling for the first time since he'd walked into the elevator.

As we tossed around the question, "What don't you know right now?" I learned that Ted doesn't know what he's going to do when he retires next year, Robin doesn't know how to play the flute, but wants to learn, and Dirk's wondering if it was such a good idea to send his daughter—a junior in college—to Costa Rica for her fall semester.

After thirty minutes, the lights in the elevator came back to full power and we could hear the hum of the elevator motor.

Ted pressed the intercom button. "Mike, are we good to go now?"

"Yup. Turns out it was only a tripped circuit breaker. Just hit your floor buttons and you're on your way. Sorry for the wait."

Ted pressed buttons four and six, the elevator began to move and we all cheered.

When our messenger friend got off at the fourth floor, Ted said, "Bye, Hank." Hank turned around, gave us a half-smile and waved as the elevator doors closed.

When the rest of us got off on the sixth floor, we headed down the main hallway toward our individual offices, still talking about our elevator adventure.

When we came to my office, I stopped outside my door and looked at my boss and colleagues. "In the thirty minutes on that elevator, I learned a lot about you guys by finding out the questions you're living with. In fact, I learned much more about you today than I did the entire week I've worked here."

After telling me about her experience, Wendy sat back in her chair, a satisfied smile on her face.

"Amazing," I said. "What a story."

"I'm glad we took time for it," she said. "That whole event was so important to me."

"And what are you left with now?"

"Well, I learned questions are like passports," Wendy said. "If you carry them with you, they take you on great adventures to new places."

My client's words were simple and wise. "Let me write *that* one down," I said, jotting myself a note.

Then I used the short time left in the session to help Wendy explore the new chapters that were unfolding in her life. She agreed to the challenge of taking it easy for the next two weeks and we ended by scheduling our next appointment.

My clients often leave their coaching sessions with inquiries to ponder...but Wendy had given *me* an inquiry that day. I still have it posted in my office:

What is it to view questions as "passports"?

INQUIRIES:

- **In a writing workshop, author Natalie Goldberg once said, "Questions are a sacred vessel." What sacred vessels are you living with right now?**
- **If questions are passports, what new territory is a current life question asking you to explore?**
- **Make a list of all the things you don't know. Invite a friend or group of friends to do the same. What do you learn about each other from sharing your lists?**

SEVEN SACRED ATTITUDES
EPILOGUE

My greatest joy in life is inviting others to wake up and take notice—to take notice of the attitudes they harbor that hold them back from the joy of bringing their gifts to the planet.

Once we notice an attitude that's holding us back, we can invite a Sacred Attitude to the party of our lives. And that's when the party really gets going.

My hope is that the essays in this collection have inspired you to **stop**, **breathe**, and **notice** when a present attitude isn't serving you well—and then to **choose** to apply a **Sacred Attitude** to your present circumstance and see what changes.

While the essays are meant to encourage your exploration and practice of the Seven Sacred Attitudes, the inquiries at the end of each essay are designed to help you deepen that process. The inquiries are worth frequent consideration.

Try opening the book at random once in a while and see what inquiries come your way. Then stick with those inquiries for a day, a month or even a year. See where you go in your life.

The essays you've just read have a vibrant life outside the

pages of this book. I select a half-dozen and read them aloud at informal gatherings of friends or clients. Afterwards, I'll pose the follow-up inquiries to the group. The resulting discussions are rich and full of life.

Try doing the same with a group of your friends, colleagues, teenagers and their friends, or with your spouse. See where you go in the discussions.

Use Inner Wisdom

Accept What's So

Go Slow

Do Less

Show Up

Trust the Process

Be With the Questions

There are endless opportunities to apply at least one of the Seven Sacred Attitudes today—and to be transformed in the process. Each and all of the Sacred Attitudes will foster meaningful action in your life and deepen your learning along the way.

But there is another Sacred Attitude to add to the top of the list. The Grandmother of all Sacred Attitudes, the sustainer of all life:

The Sacred Attitude of Love

There isn't an essay in this collection that doesn't demonstrate an element of this Sacred Attitude. It is present when we are fully present. And when we adopt the Sacred Attitude of Love, everyone on the planet benefits.

Since taking a deep breath is the way in to any of the Sacred Attitudes, I hope you find it as comforting as I do to know that a Sacred Attitude is only a breath away.

Enjoy the process.

***

If the spirit moves you, contact me through my website and let me know what you discover as you explore the Seven Sacred Attitudes. I'd enjoy hearing from you. Please contact me at:
www.EricaRossKrieger.com

SEVEN SACRED ATTITUDES ACKNOWLEDGEMENTS

A deep bow of gratitude to all of those who have contributed to my understanding of Sacred Attitudes and to the birth of this book:

To my earliest teacher of Sacred Attitudes—my mom, Barbara, who taught me to see the sacred everywhere and in everyone.

To my dad, Joe, who has been reminding me to stop and smell the roses (the *Go Slow* Attitude) ever since I can remember.

To the teachers with whom I've studied and whose work has touched my soul—cultural anthropologist and shaman, Angeles Arrien, Ph.D.; inspirational author, teacher, and friend, Dan Millman; Tai Sophia Institute founders, and teachers of acupuncture philosophy in action, Robert M. Duggan, M.Ac. (UK), M.A., and Dianne M. Connelly, Ph.D.; and dance therapist, Tamara Greenberg, ADTR.

To Gremlin-Taming® master, Rick Carson, Ph.D., for welcoming me into his Gremlin-Taming® family, graciously opening the door to unlimited possibilities and supporting me in developing my work.

To Natalie Goldberg, whose writing workshops first gave me permission to write with my "Wild Mind" and whose books inspire me to keep practicing no matter what.

To the health practitioners who nurture my own Sacred

Attitude of Health and Well-Being, I thank you for your contribution to my life and for dancing onto the pages of my essays—the late acupuncturist and minister, Hal Bailen, M.D. (1935-1991); nutritionists, Pati and Dr. Jack Caputo; Yoga teacher, Ofer Erez; masterful homeopath, Roger Morrison; acupuncturist Jenny Josephian, M.Ac.; Family Practitioner, Mary Lowen, M.D.; and Qigong Master, Roger Jahnke, O.M.D.

To Dr. Patricia Meyer, N.D., sister of my soul, who practices awesome naturopathic medicine and shows me with each visit how the Sacred Attitude of Love is the greatest healer.

To editor and agent Sue Clark, for your literary insight and foresight.

To Craig Carr, CPCC, whose brilliant coaching nurture and call me to action as I pursue my dreams, including this book, and bring them into the world. You have been a catalyst for me "to come to life more fully," in author John G. Sullivan's words.

To editor Elizabeth Day, for believing in my work, co-creating the subtitle and holding my hand through publication.

To Kevin Stock at ImageSupport, for your brilliant work, and to Todd Jacobson for your computer wizardry. Still Mountain Press could not have selected a better design team to create the book cover and layout—your art truly helps bring my words to life.

To the writers in my writing circle—Al Garotto, B. Lynn Goodwin, Bonnie Epstein, Deborah Brown, Elana O'Loskey, George Jansen, Igal Levy, Monica Emrich, Pat Mills, Pearl Schwartz, and writer/pilot Bill Lillis. To writer/colleague Charles Tack, for helping me follow the "slender threads" through the book-writing forest.

Special thanks to Peller Marion, for sharing the joys and challenges of the writing life and for all the years of unwavering friendship.

To Amy Erez, Peggy DuBois, Sally Hirst, Eileen Hammer-Housfeld, and Linda Doutre for encouragement and support along the way.

To Marney Ackerman, Chris Ebner, Eileen Giudici, Jane Holcomb, Jeanne Maltby, and Judy Nobriga for listening to the first batch of essays and inquiries. And to Contra Costa Times sportswriter, Bill Kolb, who read the book's first draft and gave me some critical baseball tips. Thank you all for your generous gifts of precious time and feedback.

To the man who I wrote about in "Waiting For Myself," whose name I do not know but whose lessons are written in my heart.

And many thanks to the coaching clients, colleagues and acquaintances whose presence in my life has illuminated the essays in this book; you will recognize yourself, even though I have concealed you in your story, changed your name, gender, age or profession or blended your story with another. You have touched my heart and your stories will now, I hope, touch the hearts of many others. Namaste.

COPYRIGHT ACKNOWLEDGEMENTS

The author and publisher gratefully acknowledge the permission to reprint selections from the previously published material listed below:

HarperCollins Publishers, for excerpts from pp. 104, 113 from *365 TAO: DAILY MEDITATIONS*, by Deng Ming-Dao. Copyright © 1992 by Deng Ming-Dao. Reprinted by permission of HarperCollins Publishers.

Jaroldeen Asplund Edwards and Shadow Mountain® Publishers, for the complete text of The *Daffodil Principle* by Jaroldeen Asplund Edwards. Copyright © 2004 by Jaroldeen Asplund Edwards. Permission granted by the author.

John G. Sullivan and the Tai Sophia Institute, for John G. Sullivan's quote (which is also the mission statement of the Master's program in Applied Healing Arts at Tai Sophia Institute, Laurel, MD). The cited quote was formulated by John G. Sullivan, the program's first director, who relied on an ancient Chinese adage pointing to the sage within and the ruler without. Used with permission by John G. Sullivan and the Tai Sophia Institute.

Tai Sophia Institute for the Healing Arts, for the complete article, "Enough Fish for the Day," from *Quintessence*, Winter, 1994. Used by permission of the publisher.

Traditional Chinese Medicine World, for the complete article, "The Crowded Alley," from *Traditional Chinese Medicine World* 4,2 (Summer 2000). Used with permission of Traditional Chinese Medicine World, New York.

SEVEN SACRED ATTITUDES

ABOUT THE AUTHOR

Erica Ross-Krieger, M.A., has been coaching individuals, groups and workplace teams for more than twenty years. A passionate advocate of self-development and living life to its fullest, she currently works with those who are struggling to achieve their personal and professional dreams.

She holds a B.A. from U.C. Berkeley in Social Welfare and an M.A. in Organizational Development from the University of San Francisco. She is a Certified Nutrition Educator and Business Coach, did her post-graduate studies in Art Therapy at U.C. Berkeley, and is trained and certified in a number of behavioral and organizational change methodologies and business assessment instruments.

Ms. Ross-Krieger is also a graduate of Coaches Training Institute, Leadership University's B/Coach programs, Angeles Arrien's Four-Fold Way program and the year-long professional training program at the Gremlin-Taming Institute™. She continues her commitment to her own professional and personal development through her on-going practice and study of Rick Carson's Gremlin-Taming Method®.

Erica blends her extensive professional background with her personal life experiences to offer programs, services and products rich with multi-faceted wisdom—in doing so, her work fosters a sense of well-being for clients and readers worldwide.

Her previous publications include: *The Wisdom of Chinese Medicine: A Powerful Paradigm for Organization Development Practitioners* and "A New Definition of Health," published in *Chicken Soup For The Body and Soul* (2004).

At present, Erica is writing and compiling essays for *Seven Sacred Attitudes® for Writers* and *Seven Sacred Attitudes® for Navigating Midlife*. If you are interested in submitting an essay, please visit her website and learn about submission requirements.

Erica resides in northern California with her husband, Steve, and a garden of lavender that soothes her soul.

Visit Erica's website and learn more about:

- Free Teleclasses and inspirational articles
- Professional and personal life coaching for individuals and small groups
- Seven Sacred Attitudes® in Action Teleclasses
- Seven Sacred Attitudes® for Writers Workshops
- Products, coaching services and an Annual Retreat designed just for writers
- Seven Sacred Attitudes® Sterling Bracelets
- Upcoming books and submission requirements for essays

www.EricaRossKrieger.com